Rich Brott

All the Financial Scriptures in the Bible

With Commentary

Published by
ABC Book Publishing

AbcBookPublishing.com
Printed in U.S.A.

All the Financial Scriptures in the Bible with Commentary
©Copyright 2008 by Richard A. Brott
10 Digit ISBN: 1-60185-004-2
13 Digit ISBN (EAN): 978-1-60185-004-1

All scripture quotations, unless otherwise indicated, are taken from the *Holy Bible, New International Version*®. *NIV*®. Copyright © 1973, 1978, 1984 by International Bible Society. Used by permission of Zondervan Publishing House. All rights reserved.

Other Versions used are:
AMP- Amplified Bible.
Amer. Std.-American Standard Version, 1901.
KJV-King James Version. Authorized King James Version.
NASB-Scripture taken from the *New American Standard Bible*, ©1960, 1962, 1963, 1968, 1971, 1972, 1973, 1975, 1977 by The Lockman Foundation. Used by permission.
Scripture taken from the *New King James Version*. Copyright © 1979, 1980, 1982 by Thomas Nelson, Inc. Publishers. Used by permission. All rights reserved.
Verses marked (*TLB*) are taken from *The Living Bible* © 1971. Used by permission of Tyndale House Publishers, Inc., Wheaton, IL 60189. All rights reserved.
Scripture taken from *THE MESSAGE: The Bible in Contemporary Language* © 2002 by Eugene H. Peterson. All rights reserved.

All rights reserved, including the right to reproduce this book, or any portions thereof, in any form. No part of this book may be reproduced or transmitted in any form or by any means, electronic or mechanical, magnetic, chemical, optical, manual, or otherwise, including photocopying, recording, or by any information storage or retrieval system without written permission from Richard A. Brott. All rights for publishing this book or portions thereof in other languages are contracted by the author.

This publication is designed to provide interesting reading material and general information with regard to the subject matter covered. It is printed, distributed and sold with the understanding that neither the publisher nor the author is engaged in rendering religious, family, legal, accounting, business, investing, financial, credit, debt or other professional advice. If any such advice is required, the services of a competent professional person should be sought. In summary, the content contained herein is not given as advice, rather it is strictly for the purpose of your reading entertainment.

Every effort has been made to supply complete and accurate information. However, neither the publisher nor the author assumes any responsibility for its use, nor for any infringements of patents or other rights of third parties that would result.

First Edition, January 1, 2008
Richard A. Brott
All Rights Reserved

About the Author

Rich Brott holds a Bachelor of Science degree in Business and Economics and a Master of Business Administration.

Rich has served in an executive position of some very successful businesses. He has functioned on the board of directors for churches, businesses, and charities and served on a college advisory board. He has traveled to more than 25 countries on teaching assignments and business concerns.

He has authored thirty-five books including:
- *5 Simple Keys to Financial Freedom*
- *10 Life-Changing Attitudes That Will Make You a Financial Success*
- *15 Biblical Responsibilities Leading to Financial Wisdom*
- *17 Biblical Principles for Receiving Supernatural Provision*
- *20 Biblical Principles for Understanding the Purpose of Financial Blessing*
- *29 Biblical Principles for Achieving Financial Alignment*
- *30 Biblical Principles for Managing Your Money*
- *35 Keys to Financial Independence*
- *A Biblical Perspective On Giving Generously*
- *A Biblical Perspective On Tithing Faithfully*
- *A Biblical Perspective On Tithing & Giving*
- *Activating Your Personal Faith to Receive*
- *All the Financial Scriptures in the Bible*
- *Basic Principles for Business Success*
- *Basic Principles for Developing Personal and Business Vision*
- *Basic Principles for Managing a Successful Business*

- *Basic Principles for Maximizing Your Personal Cash Flow*
- *Basic Principles for Starting a Successful Business*
- *Basic Principles of Conservative Investing*
- *Biblical Principles for Achieving Personal Success*
- *Biblical Principles for Becoming Debt Free*
- *Biblical Principles for Building a Successful Business*
- *Biblical Principles for Financial Success - Student Workbook*
- *Biblical Principles for Financial Success - Teacher Workbook*
- *Biblical Principles for Personal Evangelism*
- *Biblical Principles for Releasing Financial Provision*
- *Biblical Principles for Staying Out of Debt*
- *Biblical Principles for Success in Personal Finance*
- *Biblical Principles That Create Success Through Productivity*
- *Business, Occupations, Professions & Vocations In the Bible*
- *Family Finance Handbook*
- *Family Finance Student Workbook*
- *Family Finance Teacher Workbook*
- *Public Relations for the Local Church*
- *Successful Time Management*

He and his wife Karen, have been married for 35 years. Rich Brott resides in Portland, Oregon, with his wife, three children, son-in-law and granddaughter.

Dedication

This compilation of Scriptural references and commentary is dedicated to the individual and/or teacher who seeks an intimate knowledge of what the Bible has to say about financial and stewardship related topics. It provides a one-stop source for your personal study or classroom environment.

Table of Contents

About the Author 3
Dedication 5
Table of Contents 7
Introduction 9
Abundance 11
Accounting 26
Actions Against the Less Fortunate 28
Blamelessness 34
Borrowing 38
Budgeting 43
Caution 47
Contentment 50
Counsel 56
Co-signing Notes 58
Debt 61
Diligence 66
Dishonesty 70
Envy 76
Excellence 77
Getting the Facts 78
Giving 80
Greed 85
Helping the Less Fortunate 88
Hoarding & Greed 93
Honesty 96
Honesty versus Unmerited Gain 99
Humility 101
Inheritance 104
Investing 107

Investments	112
Laziness	117
Lending	121
Needs	124
Planning	126
Pride	127
Prosper	131
Prosperity	143
Prosperous	151
Retirement	153
Rich & Riches	154
Saving	163
Self-Control	165
Sharing	167
Slothfulness	171
Speculation	172
Suing	173
Supporting the Wealthy	176
Taxes	177
Tithing	179
Trust	183
Truthfulness	184
Waste	189
Wealth	192
Wives	203
Work	205
Worry	209
Offering	215
Offerings	327
Summary	333

Introduction

The Bible is packed full of Scriptures that are related in some way to financial topics. The Scriptures relate to personal stewardship, issues of debt and credit, saving and investing, how to treat the poor and less fortunate, honesty and truthfulness, laziness and diligence, contentment and the cost of self-indulgence, business and entrepreneurism, tithing and the giving of offerings, as well as wealth and abundance. So many areas of our financial life are written about in Scripture.

The Scriptures in the Bible that relate to issues of finance and stewardship offer to each of us help in many areas of our personal and professional life. With them we can learn and understand that:

- Money management is very closely related to the biblical idea of stewardship.

- We must become wise when it comes to borrowing and credit issues.

- We can live according to God's Word, and enjoy the blessings that flow out of this obedience.

- We must find out what God's purpose is for our life and for our finances.

- By living these principles they will not only affect our checkbooks, but also our priorities, our personal goals, our vision, and our lifestyle.

- It is important to learn what God has to say about money management.

- When we are successful in God's economy, we benefit both now and for eternity.

- Those who build their lives upon the truths of God's Word discover a foundation that brings peace, wisdom, and success.

"Jesus Christ said more about money than about any other single thing because, when it comes to a man's real nature, money is of first importance. Money is an exact index to a man's true character. All through Scripture, there is an intimate correlation between the development of a man's character and how he handles his money."

— Richard C. Halverson (1916-1995)
Former Senate chaplain, pastor and author

Abundance

*I*f God were to look down upon you with the idea of blessing you beyond your expectations, but first checked your money motive, what would He find? Would you be the one He can trust with great wealth, knowing you would use it to bless the kingdom of God? Or would you be the one who would simply use it to accumulate more personal possessions and to live a life of personal fulfillment and easy living? The focus of many people is pleasure, sensual indulgence, money, selfishness, power and flattery. People who live this way do nothing of lasting or eternal value. They have no ultimate purpose in mind. As Christians, we need to have eternal values and purpose.

Our motives and priorities must be God and His kingdom first, me last. Sometimes we get jealous of the success of others who are not Christians. They seem to be happy and rich and enjoying a life of luxury. A musician and prophet in Old Testament times by the name of Asaph, said, "I was envious at the foolish, when I saw the prosperity of the wicked" (Psalm 73:3).

Ungodly men and women may achieve material prosperity apart from God, but they can never achieve the deep settled peace that comes from God. Riches gained without God are a snare and do not bring peace. Prosperity that comes from God brings not only an abundance, but also emotional peace, happiness and great joy.

Genesis 27:28

Therefore may God give you of the dew of heaven, of the fatness of the earth, And plenty of grain and wine. NKJV

All the Financial Scriptures in the Bible with Commentary

Genesis 41:29

Indeed seven years of great plenty will come throughout all the land of Egypt; NKJV

Genesis 41:30-32

But after them seven years of famine will arise, and all the plenty will be forgotten in the land of Egypt; and the famine will deplete the land. So the plenty will not be known in the land because of the famine following, for it will be very severe. And the dream was repeated to Pharaoh twice because the thing is established by God, and God will shortly bring it to pass. NKJV

Genesis 41:47

Now in the seven plentiful years the ground brought forth abundantly. NKJV

Genesis 41:48

So he gathered up all the food of the seven years which were in the land of Egypt, and laid up the food in the cities; he laid up in every city the food of the fields which surrounded them. NKJV

Deuteronomy 33:19

They shall call the peoples to the mountain; there they shall offer sacrifices of righteousness; for they shall partake of the abundance of the seas and of treasures hidden in the sand." NKJV

Numbers 24:7

He shall pour water from his buckets, and his seed shall be in many waters. "His king shall be higher than Agag, and his kingdom shall be exalted. NKJV

Deuteronomy 6:3

Therefore hear, O Israel, and be careful to observe it, that it may be well with you, and that you may multiply greatly as the LORD God of your fathers has promised you — 'a land flowing with milk and honey.' NKJV

Deuteronomy 28:11

And the LORD will grant you plenty of goods, in the fruit of your body, in the increase of your livestock, and in the produce of your ground, in the land of which the LORD swore to your fathers to give you. NKJV

Deuteronomy 32:2

Let my teaching drop as the rain, my speech distill as the dew, as raindrops on the tender herb, and as showers on the grass. NKJV

1 Chronicles 29:16

O LORD our God, all this abundance that we have prepared to build You a house for Your holy name is from Your hand, and is all Your own. NKJV

1 Chronicles 29:21

And they made sacrifices to the LORD and offered burnt offerings to the LORD on the next day: a thousand bulls, a thousand rams, a thousand lambs, with their drink offerings, and sacrifices in abundance for all Israel. NKJV

2 Chronicles 11:23

He dealt wisely, and dispersed some of his sons throughout all the territories of Judah and Benjamin, to every fortified city; and he gave them provisions in abundance. He also sought many wives for them. NKJV

2 Chronicles 29:35

Also the burnt offerings were in abundance, with the fat of the peace offerings and with the drink offerings for every burnt offering. So the service of the house of the LORD was set in order. NKJV

Nehemiah 5:18

Now that which was prepared daily was one ox and six choice sheep. Also fowl were prepared for me, and once every ten days an abundance of all kinds of wine. Yet in spite of this I did not demand the governor's provisions, because the bondage was heavy on this people. NKJV

Nehemiah 9:25

And they took strong cities and a rich land, and possessed houses full of all goods, cisterns already dug, vineyards, olive groves, and fruit trees in abundance. So they ate and were filled and grew fat, and delighted themselves in Your great goodness. NKJV

Nehemiah 9:37

And it yields much increase to the kings you have set over us, because of our sins; also they have dominion over our bodies and our cattle at their pleasure; and we are in great distress. NKJV

Esther 1:7

And they served drinks in golden vessels, each vessel being different from the other, with royal wine in abundance, according to the generosity of the king. NKJV

Job 36:28

Which the clouds drop down and pour abundantly on man. NKJV

Job 36:31

For by these He judges the peoples; He gives food in abundance. NKJV

Psalms 36:8

They are abundantly satisfied with the fullness of Your house, and You give them drink from the river of Your pleasures. NKJV

Psalms 65:11

You crown the year with Your goodness, and Your paths drip with abundance. NKJV

Psalms 66:12

You have caused men to ride over our heads; we went through fire and through water; but You brought us out to rich fulfillment. NKJV

Psalms 68:9

You, O God, sent a plentiful rain, whereby You confirmed Your inheritance, when it was weary. NKJV

Abundance

Psalms 73:10

Therefore his people return here, and waters of a full cup are drained by them. NKJV

Psalms 78:15

He split the rocks in the wilderness, and gave them drink in abundance like the depths. NKJV

Psalms 132:15

I will abundantly bless her provision; I will satisfy her poor with bread. NKJV

Psalms 132:15

I will abundantly bless her provision. NKJV

Psalms 144:13

hat our barns may be full, supplying all kinds of produce; that our sheep may bring forth thousands and ten thousands in our fields; NKJV

Psalms 145:7

They shall utter the memory of Your great goodness, and shall sing of Your righteousness. NKJV

Proverbs 12:11

He who tills his land will be satisfied with bread, but he who follows frivolity is devoid of understanding. NKJV

Proverbs 13:23

Much food is in the fallow ground of the poor, and for lack of justice there is waste. NKJV

Proverbs 14:4

Where no oxen are, the trough is clean; but much increase comes by the strength of an ox. NKJV

Proverbs 20:15

There is gold and a multitude of rubies, but the lips of knowledge are a precious jewel. NKJV

Proverbs 28:19

He who tills his land will have plenty of bread, but he who follows frivolity will have poverty enough! NKJV

Ecclesiastes 5:12

The sleep of a laboring man is sweet, whether he eats little or much; but the abundance of the rich will not permit him to sleep. NKJV

Isaiah 7:22

So it shall be, from the abundance of milk they give, that he will eat curds; for curds and honey everyone will eat who is left in the land. NKJV

Isaiah 23:18

Her gain and her pay will be set apart for the LORD; it will not be treasured nor laid up, for her gain will be for those who dwell before the LORD, to eat sufficiently, and for fine clothing. NKJV

Isaiah 30:23

Then He will give the rain for your seed with which you sow the ground, and bread of the increase of the earth; it will be fat and plentiful. In that day your cattle will feed in large pastures. NKJV

Isaiah 30:33

For Tophet was established of old, yes, for the king it is prepared. He has made it deep and large; Its pyre is fire with much wood; the breath of the LORD, like a stream of brimstone, kindles it. NKJV

Isaiah 33:23

Your tackle is loosed, they could not strengthen their mast, they could not spread the sail. NKJV

Isaiah 66:11

That you may feed and be satisfied with the consolation of her bosom, that you may drink deeply and be delighted with the abundance of her glory." NKJV

Jeremiah 2:22

For though you wash yourself with lye, and use much soap, yet your iniquity is marked before Me," says the Lord GOD. NKJV

Jeremiah 31:14

I will satiate the soul of the priests with abundance, and My people shall be satisfied with My goodness, says the LORD." NKJV

Jeremiah 33:6

Behold, I will bring it health and healing; I will heal them and reveal to them the abundance of peace and truth. NKJV

Jeremiah 33:9

Then it shall be to Me a name of joy, a praise, and an honor before all nations of the earth, who shall hear all the good that I do to them; they shall fear and tremble for all the goodness and all the prosperity that I provide for it.' NKJV

Jeremiah 40:12

Then all the Jews returned out of all places where they had been driven, and came to the land of Judah, to Gedaliah at Mizpah, and gathered wine and summer fruit in abundance. NKJV

Ezekiel 17:5

Then he took some of the seed of the land and planted it in a fertile field; He placed it by abundant waters and set it like a willow tree. NKJV

Ezekiel 17:8

It was planted in good soil by many waters, to bring forth branches, bear fruit, and become a majestic vine. NKJV

Ezekiel 19:10

Your mother was like a vine in your bloodline, planted by the waters, fruitful and full of branches because of many waters. NKJV

Ezekiel 31:5

Therefore its height was exalted above all the trees of the field; Its boughs were multiplied, and its branches became long because of the abundance of water, as it sent them out. NKJV

Ezekiel 31:7

Thus it was beautiful in greatness and in the length of its branches, because its roots reached to abundant waters. NKJV

Ezekiel 31:9

I made it beautiful with a multitude of branches, so that all the trees of Eden envied it, that were in the garden of God.' NKJV

Ezekiel 31:15

Thus says the Lord GOD: 'In the day when it went down to hell, I caused mourning. I covered the deep because of it. I restrained its rivers, and the great waters were held back. I caused Lebanon to mourn for it, and all the trees of the field wilted because of it. NKJV

Ezekiel 32:13

Also I will destroy all its animals from beside its great waters; the foot of man shall muddy them no more, nor shall the hooves of animals muddy them. NKJV

Ezekiel 32:15

When I make the land of Egypt desolate, and the country is destitute of all that once filled it, when I strike all who dwell in it, then they shall know that I am the LORD. NKJV

Daniel 4:12

Its leaves were lovely, its fruit abundant, and in it was food for all. The beasts of the field found shade under it, the birds of the heavens dwelt in its branches, and all flesh was fed from it. NKJV

Daniel 4:21

whose leaves were lovely and its fruit abundant, in which was food for all, under which the beasts of the field dwelt, and in whose branches the birds of the heaven had their home — NKJV

Joel 2:23

Be glad then, you children of Zion, and rejoice in the LORD your God; for He has given you the former rain faithfully, and He will cause the rain to come down for you – the former rain, and the latter rain in the first month. NKJV

Matthew 13:12

For whoever has, to him more will be given, and he will have abundance; but whoever does not have, even what he has will be taken away from him. NKJV

Matthew 25:29

'For to everyone who has, more will be given, and he will have abundance; but from him who does not have, even what he has will be taken away. NKJV

Luke 12:15

And He said to them, "Take heed and beware of covetousness, for one's life does not consist in the abundance of the things he possesses." NKJV

Luke 21:4

For all these out of their abundance have put in offerings for God, but she out of her poverty put in all the livelihood that she had." NKJV

John 10:10

The thief does not come except to steal, and to kill, and to destroy. I have come that they may have life, and that they may have it more abundantly. NKJV

John 15:5

"I am the vine, you are the branches. He who abides in Me, and I in him, bears much fruit; for without Me you can do nothing. NKJV

Romans 5:17

For if by the one man's offense death reigned through the one, much more those who receive abundance of grace and of the gift of righteousness will reign in life through the One, Jesus Christ.) NKJV

2 Corinthians 9:8

And God is able to make all grace abound toward you, that you, always having all sufficiency in all things, may have an abundance for every good work. NKJV

Philippians 4:12

I know how to be abased, and I know how to abound. Everywhere and in all things I have learned both to be full and to be hungry, both to abound and to suffer need. NKJV

1 Peter 1:2

Elect according to the foreknowledge of God the Father, in sanctification of the Spirit, for obedience and sprinkling of the blood of Jesus Christ: Grace to you and peace be multiplied. NKJV

2 Peter 1:2

Grace and peace be multiplied to you in the knowledge of God and of Jesus our Lord, NKJV

Jude 2

Mercy, peace, and love be multiplied to you. NKJV

Accounting

Daniel 6:1-2

It pleased Darius to appoint 120 satraps to rule throughout the kingdom, with three administrators over them, one of whom was Daniel. The satraps were made accountable to them so that the king might not suffer loss. NIV

Matthew 18:23

Therefore, the kingdom of heaven is like a king who wanted to settle accounts with his servants. NIV

Matthew 25:14-30

Again, it will be like a man going on a journey, who called his servants and entrusted his property to them. To one he gave five talents of money, to another two talents, and to another one talent, each according to his ability. Then he went on his journey. The man who had received the five talents went at once and put his money to work and gained five more. So also, the one with the two talents gained two more. But the man who had received the one talent went off, dug a hole in the ground and hid his master's money. "After a long time the master of those servants returned and settled accounts with them. The man who had received the five talents brought the other five. 'Master,' he said, 'you entrusted me with five talents. See, I have gained five more.' "His master replied, 'Well done, good and faithful servant!

You have been faithful with a few things; I will put you in charge of many things. Come and share your master's happiness!" "The man with the two talents also came. 'Master,' he said, 'you entrusted me with two talents; see, I have gained two more.' "His master replied, 'Well done, good and faithful servant! You have been faithful with a few things; I will put you in charge of many things. Come and share your master's happiness!" "Then the man who had received the one talent came. 'Master,' he said, 'I knew that you are a hard man, harvesting where you have not sown and gathering where you have not scattered seed. So I was afraid and went out and hid your talent in the ground. See, here is what belongs to you.' "His master replied, 'You wicked, lazy servant! So you knew that I harvest where I have not sown and gather where I have not scattered seed? Well then, you should have put my money on deposit with the bankers, so that when I returned I would have received it back with interest. "'Take the talent from him and give it to the one who has the ten talents. For everyone who has will be given more, and he will have an abundance. Whoever does not have, even what he has will be taken from him. And throw that worthless servant outside, into the darkness, where there will be weeping and gnashing of teeth.' NIV

Romans 14:12

So then, each of us will give an account of himself to God. NIV

Actions Against the Less Fortunate

Deuteronomy 24:14

You shall not oppress a hired servant who is poor and needy, whether he is one of your countrymen or one of your aliens who is in your land in your towns. NASB

Psalms 10:2

In pride the wicked hotly pursue the afflicted;

Let them be caught in the plots which they have devised. NASB

Psalms 12:5

Because of the devastation of the afflicted, because of the groaning of the needy, now I will arise," says the LORD; "I will set him in the safety for which he longs." NASB

Proverbs 14:20-21, 31

The poor is hated even by his neighbor, but those who love the rich are many. He who despises his neighbor sins, but happy is he who is gracious to the poor. He who oppresses the poor reproaches his Maker, but he who is gracious to the needy honors Him. NASB

Actions Against the Less Fortunate

Proverbs 21:13

He who shuts his ear to the cry of the poor will also cry himself and not be answered. NASB

Proverbs 22:16

He who oppresses the poor to make much for himself or who gives to the rich, will only come to poverty. NASB

Proverbs 24:23

These also are sayings of the wise. To show partiality in judgment is not good. NASB

Proverbs 28:8

He who increases his wealth by interest and usury, gathers it for him who is gracious to the poor. NASB

Matthew 18:23, 34

For this reason the kingdom of heaven may be compared to a certain king who wished to settle accounts with his slaves. And his lord, moved with anger, handed him over to the torturers until he should repay all that was owed him. NASB

Luke 11:42

But woe to you Pharisees! For you pay tithe of mint and rue and every kind of garden herb, and yet disregard justice and the love of God; but these are the things you should have done without neglecting the others. NASB

Luke 16:19-25

Now there was a certain rich man, and he habitually dressed in purple and fine linen, gaily living in splendor every day. And a certain poor man named Lazarus was laid at his gate, covered with sores, and longing to be fed with the crumbs which were falling from the rich man's table; besides, even the dogs were coming and licking his sores. Now it came about that the poor man died and he was carried away by the angels to Abraham's bosom; and the rich man also died and was buried. And in Hades he lifted up his eyes, being in torment, and saw Abraham far away, and Lazarus in his bosom. And he cried out and said, 'Father Abraham, have mercy on me, and send Lazarus, that he may dip the tip of his finger in water and cool off my tongue; for I am in agony in this flame.' But Abraham said, 'Child, remember that during your life you received your good things, and likewise Lazarus bad things; but now he is being comforted here, and you are in agony NASB

Attitudes, Viewpoints & Actions

Psalm 112:2-3

His descendants will be mighty on earth; the generation of the upright will be blessed. Wealth and riches are in his house, and his righteousness endures forever. NASB

Psalm 112:9

He has given freely to the poor, His righteousness endures forever; His horn will be exalted in honor. NASB

Proverbs 10:4

Poor is he who works with a negligent hand, but the hand of the diligent makes rich. NASB

Proverbs 13:4, 11

The soul of the sluggard craves and gets nothing, but the soul of the diligent is made fat. Wealth obtained by fraud dwindles, but the one who gathers by labor increases it. NASB

Proverbs 24:10

If you are slack in the day of distress, your strength is limited. NASB

Prov 28:27

He who gives to the poor will never want, But he who shuts his eyes will have many curses. NASB

Eccl 5:12

The sleep of the working man is pleasant, whether he eats little or much. But the full stomach of the rich man does not allow him to sleep. NASB

Mal 3:5-6

"Then I will draw near to you for judgment; and I will be a swift witness against the sorcerers and against the adulterers and against those who swear falsely, and against those who oppress the wage earner in his wages, the widow and the orphan, and those who turn aside the alien, and do not fear Me," says the LORD of hosts. NASB

Luke 6:35

But love your enemies, and do good, and lend, expecting nothing in return; NASB

Rom 12:11

not lagging behind in diligence, fervent in spirit, serving the Lord; NASB

Eph 4:28

Let him who steals steal no longer; but rather let him labor, performing with his own hands what is good, in order that he may have something to share with him who has need. NASB

Blamelessness

Psalm 1:1, 2

Blessed is the man who does not walk in the counsel of the wicked or stand in the way of sinners or sit in the seat of mockers. But his delight is in the law of the LORD, and on his law he meditates day and night. NIV

Psalm 37:37

Consider the blameless, observe the upright; there is a future for the man of peace. NIV

Psalm 112:6

Surely he will never be shaken; a righteous man will be remembered forever. NIV

Proverbs 10:16

The wages of the righteous bring them life, but the income of the wicked brings them punishment. NIV

Proverbs 11:4

Wealth is worthless in the day of wrath, but righteousness delivers from death. NIV

Proverbs 12:12

The wicked desire the plunder of evil men, but the root of the righteous flourishes. NIV

Proverbs 16:8, 11

Better a little with righteousness than much gain with injustice. Honest scales and balances are from the LORD; all the weights in the bag are of his making. NIV

Proverbs 19:1

Better a poor man whose walk is blameless than a fool whose lips are perverse. NIV

Proverbs 21:3

To do what is right and just is more acceptable to the LORD than sacrifice. NIV

Proverbs 22:1

A good name is more desirable than great riches; to be esteemed is better than silver or gold. NIV

Proverbs 28:6, 13

Better a poor man whose walk is blameless than a rich man whose ways are perverse. He who conceals his sins does not prosper, but whoever confesses and renounces them finds mercy. NIV

Matthew 7:20

Thus, by their fruit you will recognize them. NIV

Luke 3:12-14

Tax collectors also came to be baptized. "Teacher," they asked, "what should we do?" "Don't collect any more than you are required to," he told them. Then some soldiers asked him, "And what should we do?" He replied, "Don't extort money and don't accuse people falsely-be content with your pay." NIV

Luke 8:15

But the seed on good soil stands for those with a noble and good heart, who hear the word, retain it, and by persevering produce a crop. NIV

Luke 12:57, 58

Why don't you judge for yourselves what is right? As you are going with your adversary to the magistrate, try hard to be reconciled to him on the way, or he may drag you off to the judge, and the judge turn you over to the officer, and the officer throw you into prison. NIV

Luke 20:22-25

Is it right for us to pay taxes to Caesar or not?" He saw through their duplicity and said to them, "Show me a denarius. Whose portrait and inscription are on it?" "Caesar's," they replied. He said to them, "Then give to Caesar what is Caesar's, and to God what is God's." NIV

Romans 13:7

Give everyone what you owe him: If you owe taxes, pay taxes; if revenue, then revenue; if respect, then respect; if honor, then honor. NIV

Galatians 6:9

Let us not become weary in doing good, for at the proper time we will reap a harvest if we do not give up. NIV

Borrowing

Too often, people are quick to borrow instead of trusting the Lord to meet their needs. After all, doesn't Scripture tell us that our God is a providing God, and that He will take care of us by meeting our needs? What if we turn to credit and take on new debt, when all along God wanted to show Himself strong on our behalf? Before you run to the bank for a loan, before you pull out the charge card, before you rush to meet your own needs, give time for the provision of God to work.

> *"Not that I am looking for a gift, but I am looking for what may be credited to your account. I have received full payment and even more; I am amply supplied, now that I have received from Epaphroditus the gifts you sent. They are a fragrant offering, an acceptable sacrifice, pleasing to God. And my God will meet all your needs according to His glorious riches in Christ Jesus"* (Philippians 4:17-19 NIV).

We have been taught from childhood to make decisions and move quickly and decisively, so we feel compelled to hurry to fix our own problems. Yet, in spite of this need for speed, we should be patient in waiting on God. We should be cautious about always making our own way independently instead of seeking the wisdom of God.

Ex 22:14

And if a man borrows anything from his neighbor, and it becomes injured or dies, the owner of it not being with it, he shall surely make it good. NKJV

Deuteronomy 15:1-11

At the end of every seven years you shall grant a release of debts. And this is the form of the release: Every creditor who has lent anything to his neighbor shall release it; he shall not require it of his neighbor or his brother, because it is called the LORD's release. Of a foreigner you may require it; but you shall give up your claim to what is owed by your brother, except when there may be no poor among you; for the LORD will greatly bless you in the land which the LORD your God is giving you to possess as an inheritance— only if you carefully obey the voice of the LORD your God, to observe with care all these commandments which I command you today. For the LORD your God will bless you just as He promised you; you shall lend to many nations, but you shall not borrow; you shall reign over many nations, but they shall not reign over you. If there is among you a poor man of your brethren, within any of the gates in your land which the LORD your God is giving you, you shall not harden your heart nor shut your hand from your poor brother, but you shall open your hand wide to him and willingly lend him sufficient for his need, whatever he needs. Beware lest there be a wicked thought in your heart, saying, 'The seventh year, the year of release, is at hand,' and your eye be evil against your poor brother and you give him nothing, and he cry out to the LORD against you, and it become sin among you. You shall surely give to him, and your heart should not be grieved when you give to him, because for this thing the LORD your God will bless you in all your works and in all to which you put your hand. For the poor will never cease from the land; therefore I command you, saying, 'You shall open your hand wide to your brother, to your poor and your needy, in your land.' If your brother, a Hebrew man, or a Hebrew woman, is sold to you and serves you six years, then in the seventh year you shall let him go free from you. And when you send him away free from you, you shall not let him go away empty-handed; you shall supply him liberally from your flock, from your threshing floor, and from your winepress. From what the LORD your God has blessed you with, you shall give to him. You shall remember that you were a slave in the land of Egypt, and the LORD your God redeemed you; therefore I command you this thing today. NKJV

Ps 37:25

I have been young, and now am old; yet I have not seen the righteous forsaken, nor his descendants begging bread. NKJV

Prov 3:27-28

Do not withhold good from those to whom it is due, when it is in the power of your hand to do so. Do not say to your neighbor, "Go, and come back, and tomorrow I will give it," NKJV

Prov 22:7

The rich rules over the poor, and the borrower is servant to the lender. NKJV

Matt 5:25-26, 40

Agree with your adversary quickly, while you are on the way with him, lest your adversary deliver you to the judge, the judge hand you over to the officer, and you be thrown into prison. Assuredly, I say to you, you will by no means get out of there till you have paid the last penny. If anyone wants to sue you and take away your tunic, let him have your cloak also. NKJV

Matt 18:23-35

Therefore the kingdom of heaven is like a certain king who wanted to settle accounts with his servants. And when he had begun to settle accounts, one was brought to him who owed him ten thousand talents. But as he was not able to pay, his master commanded that he be sold, with his wife and children and all that he had, and that payment be made. The servant therefore fell down before him, saying, 'Master, have patience with me, and I will pay you all.' Then the master of that servant was moved with compassion, released him, and forgave him the debt. "But that servant went out and found one of his fellow servants who owed him a hundred denarii; and he laid hands on him and took him by the throat, saying, 'Pay me what you owe!' So his fellow servant fell down at his feet and begged him, saying, 'Have patience with me, and I will pay you all.' And he would not, but went and threw him into prison till he should pay the debt. So when his fellow servants saw what had been done, they were very grieved, and came and told their master all that had been done. Then his master, after he had called him, said to him, 'You wicked servant! I forgave you all that debt because you begged me. Should you not also have had compassion on your fellow servant, just as I had pity on you?' And his master was angry, and delivered him to the torturers until he should pay all that was due to him. "So My heavenly Father also will do to you if each of you, from his heart, does not forgive his brother his trespasses." NKJV

Luke 12:58-59

When you go with your adversary to the magistrate, make every effort along the way to settle with him, lest he drag you to the judge, the judge deliver you to the officer, and the officer throw you into prison. I tell you, you shall not depart from there till you have paid the very last mite." NKJV

Budgeting

Like it or not, money is an important part of our lives. While it is true that money cannot buy happiness, it is also true that when it comes to spending more than we earn, the lack of money can contribute to much unhappiness.

If properly managed, money can enhance family relationships and can be a springboard for family discussions that will help the entire family pull together for common goals. Not properly managed, money potentially, can become a real curse.

Budgeting is Scriptural. Scriptural guidelines for budgeting can be found throughout God's Word. For instance, Proverbs 27:23 says, "Know well the condition of your flocks, and pay attention to your herds." (NASU) If you don't happen to have any herds and flocks, God is probably saying, "Know well the condition of your clothing budget, your housing budget and your food budget."

Prov 16:9

We can make our plans, but the LORD determines our steps. NLT

Prov 19:21

You can make many plans, but the LORD's purpose will prevail. NLT

Prov 22:3

A prudent person foresees the danger ahead and takes precautions; the simpleton goes blindly on and suffers the consequences. NLT

Prov 24:3-4

A house is built by wisdom and becomes strong through good sense. 4 Through knowledge its rooms are filled with all sorts of precious riches and valuables. NLT

Prov 27:12

A prudent person foresees the danger ahead and takes precautions. The simpleton goes blindly on and suffers the consequences. NLT

Luke 12:16-21

And he gave an illustration: "A rich man had a fertile farm that produced fine crops. In fact, his barns were full to overflowing. So he said, 'I know! I'll tear down my barns and build bigger ones. Then I'll have room enough to store everything. And I'll sit back and say to myself, My friend, you have enough stored away for years to come. Now take it easy! Eat, drink, and be merry!' But God said to him, 'You fool! You will die this very night. Then who will get it all?' "Yes, a person is a fool to store up earthly wealth but not have a rich relationship with God." NLT

Budgeting

Luke 14:28-30

But don't begin until you count the cost. For who would begin construction of a building without first getting estimates and then checking to see if there is enough money to pay the bills? Otherwise, you might complete only the foundation before running out of funds. And then how everyone would laugh at you! They would say, 'There's the person who started that building and ran out of money before it was finished!' NLT

Luke 16:1-8

Jesus told this story to his disciples: "A rich man hired a manager to handle his affairs, but soon a rumor went around that the manager was thoroughly dishonest. So his employer called him in and said, 'What's this I hear about your stealing from me? Get your report in order, because you are going to be dismissed.' "The manager thought to himself, 'Now what? I'm through here, and I don't have the strength to go out and dig ditches, and I'm too proud to beg. I know just the thing! And then I'll have plenty of friends to take care of me when I leave!' "So he invited each person who owed money to his employer to come and discuss the situation. He asked the first one, 'How much do you owe him?' The man replied, 'I owe him eight hundred gallons of olive oil.' So the manager told him, 'Tear up that bill and write another one for four hundred gallons.' " 'And how much do you owe my employer?' he asked the next man. 'A thousand bushels of wheat,' was the reply. 'Here,' the manager said, 'take your bill and replace it with one for only eight hundred bushels.' "The rich man had to admire the dishonest rascal for being so shrewd. And it is true that the citizens of this world are more shrewd than the godly are. NLT

1 Corinthians 16:1, 2

Now regarding your question about the money being collected for God's people in Jerusalem. You should follow the same procedure I gave to the churches in Galatia. On the first day of each week, you should each put aside a portion of the money you have earned. Don't wait until I get there and then try to collect it all at once. NLT

Caution

Proverbs 8:12

I, Wisdom, live together with good judgment. I know where to discover knowledge and discernment. NLT

Proverbs 12:16, 23

A fool is quick-tempered, but a wise person stays calm when insulted. Wise people don't make a show of their knowledge, but fools broadcast their folly. NLT

Proverbs 13:16

Wise people think before they act; fools don't and even brag about it! NLT

Proverbs 14:8, 15, 18

The wise look ahead to see what is coming, but fools deceive themselves. 15 Only simpletons believe everything they are told! The prudent carefully consider their steps. The simpleton is clothed with folly, but the wise person is crowned with knowledge. NLT

Proverbs 15:5

Only a fool despises a parent's discipline; whoever learns from correction is wise. NLT

Proverbs 16:21

The wise are known for their understanding, and instruction is appreciated if it's well presented. NLT

Proverbs 18:15

Intelligent people are always open to new ideas. In fact, they look for them. NLT

Proverbs 22:3

A prudent person foresees the danger ahead and takes precautions; the simpleton goes blindly on and suffers the consequences. NLT

Proverbs 27:12

A prudent person foresees the danger ahead and takes precautions. The simpleton goes blindly on and suffers the consequences. NLT

Hosea 14:9

Let those who are wise understand these things. Let those who are discerning listen carefully. The paths of the LORD are true and right, and righteous people live by walking in them. But sinners stumble and fall along the way. NLT

Amos 5:13

So those who are wise will keep quiet, for it is an evil time. NLT

Contentment

1 Timothy 6:8

"But if we have food and clothing, we will be content with that."

Millions of people today are on a quest to accumulate possessions and wealth. It is hard to be content with what we have when the world's entire system is geared toward making us unhappy with everything we have and wanting everything we don't have. From advertising to attitude, we face a discontented culture. How much money does it take to be content? Usually just a little bit more. Money cannot buy contentment or happiness. It is hard for us to be satisfied with what we do have, but we need to strive for contentment and contend for happiness.

Making money is certainly not wrong, as long as it does not violate the laws of our land and the principles of God's Word. The all-for-me and none-for-others way of man's thinking is immoral. People of principle who subscribe to the values of the Bible will be good stewards if they obey the law of giving. They will find happiness in exact proportion to the degree in which they give. They will be content with life and all that it affords.

Money and happiness are not mutually exclusive. Benjamin Franklin noted, "Money never made a man happy yet, nor will it. There is nothing in its nature to produce happiness. The more a man has, the more he wants. Instead of filling a vacuum, it makes one." He also said, "Contentment makes poor men rich; discontentment makes rich men poor."

Being a good steward begins with the blessing of God, but the test and fruit of good stewardship is how we use those blessings. Are we a conduit or do we stop the stream of God's favor. Do we allow the river to flow, or do we dam up God's supply? To me it is a matter of management, not ownership. Are we to give only a little and hoard the rest for our own pleasure? I think not. God expects us to use what we need (He has promised to supply our needs), then to multiply and return the rest. Stewardship is trust, knowing and disbursing His blessing. The blessing of stewardship is in giving.

Many wealthy people wish they had friends. Some of the most prominent people in the world are some of the saddest people on earth. Even their money cannot hide their unhappiness and displeasure with life. It is sad when people spend an entire lifetime trying to get rich, only to find that when they finally become rich, they are still unhappy, still dissatisfied with life and still sad.

Jesus let us know in Luke 12:15 that a person's life and happiness do not consist of things, possessions and money. In other words, all the possessions in the world will not bring contentment, nor will they buy happiness.

When the rich man in Luke 12:19 declared that after working hard for many years, accumulating great wealth and all the goods his world could offer him, he could now be free to take it easy by eating, drinking and be merry. He had dedicated his whole life to accumulating great possessions for such a time as this. Jesus called this man a fool because of his thinking. His thinking was wrong, his priorities were wrong and because of wrong thinking, he was unable to be the kind of good steward he was required to be.

The Christian is not to love money. He is to love God. The Scripture is not so much concerned about our having wealth, but is concerned with how it is obtained and how it is managed. God allows us to be partners with Him. God's role in the partnership is to meet our needs (Philippians 4:19). Our role in the partnership is to work (2 Thessalonians. 3:10). Our work is a means of worship and ministry. When we work, we meet the needs of our family and serve the Lord at the same time. We are also to work with proper motives (Colossians 3:23,24).

The rich man, whom Jesus called a fool, was an example of a person who loved money more than life itself. But God had other plans for him. After calling the man a fool and after working selfishly for a lifetime just so he could retire in pleasure and ease, God said that tonight was his last evening on earth.

Joshua 7:7-8

Then Joshua cried out, "Sovereign LORD, why did you bring us across the Jordan River if you are going to let the Amorites kill us? If only we had been content to stay on the other side! Lord, what am I to say, now that Israel has fled from its enemies? NLT

Proverbs 30:7-9

O God, I beg two favors from you before I die. First, help me never to tell a lie. Second, give me neither poverty nor riches! Give me just enough to satisfy my needs. For if I grow rich, I may deny you and say, "Who is the LORD?" And if I am too poor, I may steal and thus insult God's holy name. NLT

Matthew 20:1-16

For the Kingdom of Heaven is like the owner of an estate who went out early one morning to hire workers for his vineyard. He agreed to pay the normal daily wage and sent them out to work. At nine o'clock in the morning he was passing through the marketplace and saw some people standing around doing nothing. So he hired them, telling them he would pay them whatever was right at the end of the day. At noon and again around three o'clock he did the same thing. At five o'clock that evening he was in town again and saw some more people standing around. He asked them, 'Why haven't you been working today?' They replied, 'Because no one hired us.' "*The owner of the estate told them, 'Then go on out and join the others in my vineyard.' That evening he told the foreman to call the workers in and pay them, beginning with the last workers first. When those hired at five o'clock were paid, each received a full day's wage. When those hired earlier came to get their pay, they assumed they would receive more. But they, too, were paid a day's wage. When they received their pay, they protested, 'Those people worked only one hour, and yet you've paid them just as much as you paid us who worked all day in the scorching heat.' He answered one of them, 'Friend, I haven't been unfair! Didn't you agree to work all day for the usual wage? Take it and go. I wanted to pay this last worker the same as you. Is it against the law for me to do what I want with my money? Should you be angry because I am kind?' And so it is, that many who are first now will be last then; and those who are last now will be first then.*" NLT

Luke 3:14

"What should we do?" asked some soldiers. John replied, "Don't extort money, and don't accuse people of things you know they didn't do. And be content with your pay." NLT

Luke 12:15-21

Then he said, "Beware! Don't be greedy for what you don't have. Real life is not measured by how much we own." And he gave an illustration: "A rich man had a fertile farm that produced fine crops. In fact, his barns were full to overflowing. So he said, 'I know! I'll tear down my barns and build bigger ones. Then I'll have room enough to store everything. And I'll sit back and say to myself, My friend, you have enough stored away for years to come. Now take it easy! Eat, drink, and be merry!' But God said to him, 'You fool! You will die this very night. Then who will get it all?' "Yes, a person is a fool to store up earthly wealth but not have a rich relationship with God." NLT

2 Corinthians 6:10

Our hearts ache, but we always have joy. We are poor, but we give spiritual riches to others. We own nothing, and yet we have everything. NLT

Philippians 4:10-12

Not that I was ever in need, for I have learned how to get along happily whether I have much or little. I know how to live on almost nothing or with everything. I have learned the secret of living in every situation, whether it is with a full stomach or empty, with plenty or little. NLT

Colossians 3:2

Let heaven fill your thoughts. Do not think only about things down here on earth. NLT

1 Thessalonians 5:16-18

Always be joyful. Keep on praying. No matter what happens, always be thankful, for this is God's will for you who belong to Christ Jesus. NLT

1 Timothy 6:6-10

Yet true religion with contentment is great wealth. After all, we didn't bring anything with us when we came into the world, and we certainly cannot carry anything with us when we die. So if we have enough food and clothing, let us be content. But people who long to be rich fall into temptation and are trapped by many foolish and harmful desires that plunge them into ruin and destruction. For the love of money is at the root of all kinds of evil. And some people, craving money, have wandered from the faith and pierced themselves with many sorrows. NLT

Hebrews 13:5

Stay away from the love of money; be satisfied with what you have. For God has said, "I will never fail you. I will never forsake you." NLT

Counsel

Proverbs 3:13

Happy is the man who finds wisdom, and the man who gains understanding; NKJV

Proverbs 12:5, 15

The thoughts of the righteous are right, but the counsels of the wicked are deceitful. The way of a fool is right in his own eyes, But he who heeds counsel is wise. NKJV

Proverbs 13:20

He who walks with wise men will be wise, but the companion of fools will be destroyed. NKJV

Proverbs 14:7

Go from the presence of a foolish man, when you do not perceive in him the lips of knowledge. NKJV

Proverbs 15:22

Without counsel, plans go awry, but in the multitude of counselors they are established. NKJV

Proverbs 19:20

Listen to counsel and receive instruction, that you may be wise in your latter days. NKJV

Proverbs 24:3, 6

Through wisdom a house is built, and by understanding it is established; For by wise counsel you will wage your own war, And in a multitude of counselors there is safety. NKJV

Proverbs 27:9

Ointment and perfume delight the heart, and the sweetness of a man's friend gives delight by hearty counsel. NKJV

Co-signing Notes

One huge area of financial vulnerability is co-signing someone else's loan. Co-signing is essentially a quick way to go into debt. People who co-sign feel that they are doing a relative or friend a favor. The potential cost of their signature is usually not explained very carefully to them. When you co-sign a note, you are taking on someone else's debt. Rarely do you know just how much and what kind of debt that person may have. Debt is an excess of liabilities over assets.

A home, if financed conservatively, may usually be sold for more than is owed by the mortgagor. A car, furniture and almost all other depreciating items purchased on time cannot usually be sold for sufficient money to pay off the lender. This is often the kind of debt for which co-signers are asked to be involved.

There is always the possibility that what you co-sign for could be repossessed, leaving you still on the hook for most of the outstanding loan. Ask any credit union or bank how they come out financially when goods are repossessed. Repossession is usually a financial disaster for both the borrower and the lender.

In a given situation, the co-signer may feel some embarrassment at quizzing the lender about what will happen if his relative or friend does not pay as he has promised.

What are you doing if you co-sign a note? You need to understand the financial transaction in which you would involve yourself. Here are three factors:

1. You are borrowing the money. The lender has refused to make the loan to the person for whom you are co-signing, based on facts which reveal that the risk is too great to loan the money to your friend or relative.

When you sign the note, the money is really being loaned to you. The reason you have been asked to sign is that your collateral, your character, your credit and your capacity are sufficient for the loan officer to feel good about the security on the loan. Your signature is the loaner's security.

2. You are loaning the money. You are loaning the money you borrowed to a person who was too great a risk for the professional lender. You are involving yourself in a business transaction that the expert money manager would not touch.

3. You are hoping your friend will pay back the loan. There's a good chance that it will not happen. When your friend or relative defaults, then you have the privilege of paying back the money. Never co-sign a note unless you can afford to give the money away!

Proverbs 6:1-5

My son, if you have put up security for your neighbor, if you have struck hands in pledge for another, if you have been trapped by what you said, ensnared by the words of your mouth, then do this, my son, to free yourself, since you have fallen into your neighbor's hands: Go and humble yourself; press your plea with your neighbor! Allow no sleep to your eyes, no slumber to your eyelids. Free yourself, like a gazelle from the hand of the hunter, like a bird from the snare of the fowler. NIV

Proverbs 11:15

He who puts up security for another will surely suffer, but whoever refuses to strike hands in pledge is safe. NIV

Proverbs 17:18

A man lacking in judgment strikes hands in pledge and puts up security for his neighbor. NIV

Proverbs 20:16

Take the garment of one who puts up security for a stranger; hold it in pledge if he does it for a wayward woman. NIV

Proverbs 22:26

Do not be a man who strikes hands in pledge or puts up security for debts; NIV

Proverbs 27:13

Take the garment of one who puts up security for a stranger; hold it in pledge if he does it for a wayward woman. NIV

Debt

There is a great danger in our society of getting trapped by debt. Perhaps the greatest need in families today is to understand the consequences of being trapped by debt, with limited income, creating a financial position where recovery seems impossible.

The road into the misuse of credit is wide, broad, simple, easy, accessible, effortless, uncomplicated, painless, spacious, available and trouble-free. However there is no quick and easy way out from under a heavy debt load.

With debt, you essentially slide in and climb out. Easy to get in, difficult to get out. If you have ever been heavily in debt and burdened down with monthly payments so steep that you could barely keep your head above water and then had to slowly and methodically climb out, then you know that it is an uphill struggle. There is no easy way out. You cannot wave a magic wand and undo in twelve months what it took twelve years to accomplish.

Deuteronomy 15:6

For the LORD your God will bless you as he has promised, and you will lend to many nations but will borrow from none. You will rule over many nations but none will rule over you. NIV

Deuteronomy 28:12, 13

The LORD will open the heavens, the storehouse of his bounty, to send rain on your land in season and to bless all the work of your hands. You will lend to many nations but will borrow from none. The LORD will make you the head, not the tail. If you pay attention to the commands of the LORD your God that I give you this day and carefully follow them, you will always be at the top, never at the bottom. NIV

2 Kings 4:1-7

The wife of a man from the company of the prophets cried out to Elisha, "Your servant my husband is dead, and you know that he revered the LORD. But now his creditor is coming to take my two boys as his slaves." Elisha replied to her, "How can I help you? Tell me, what do you have in your house?" "Your servant has nothing there at all," she said, "except a little oil." Elisha said, "Go around and ask all your neighbors for empty jars. Don't ask for just a few. Then go inside and shut the door behind you and your sons. Pour oil into all the jars, and as each is filled, put it to one side." She left him and afterward shut the door behind her and her sons. They brought the jars to her and she kept pouring. When all the jars were full, she said to her son, "Bring me another one." But he replied, "There is not a jar left." Then the oil stopped flowing. She went and told the man of God, and he said, "Go, sell the oil and pay your debts. You and your sons can live on what is left." NIV

Psalm 37:21

The wicked borrow and do not repay, but the righteous give generously; NIV

Proverbs 3:27, 28

Do not withhold good from those who deserve it, when it is in your power to act. Do not say to your neighbor, "Come back later; I'll give it tomorrow" — when you now have it with you. NIV

Proverbs 6:1-3

My son, if you have put up security for your neighbor, if you have struck hands in pledge for another, if you have been trapped by what you said, ensnared by the words of your mouth, then do this, my son, to free yourself, since you have fallen into your neighbor's hands: Go and humble yourself; press your plea with your neighbor! NIV

Proverbs 11:15

He who puts up security for another will surely suffer, but whoever refuses to strike hands in pledge is safe. NIV

Proverbs 17:18

A man lacking in judgment strikes hands in pledge and puts up security for his neighbor. NIV

Proverbs 22:7

The rich rule over the poor, and the borrower is servant to the lender. NIV

Proverbs 27:13

Take the garment of one who puts up security for a stranger; hold it in pledge if he does it for a wayward woman. NIV

Matthew 5:25, 26

Settle matters quickly with your adversary who is taking you to court. Do it while you are still with him on the way, or he may hand you over to the judge, and the judge may hand you over to the officer, and you may be thrown into prison. I tell you the truth, you will not get out until you have paid the last penny. NIV

Matthew 18:23

Therefore, the kingdom of heaven is like a king who wanted to settle accounts with his servants. NIV

Luke 12:58, 59

As you are going with your adversary to the magistrate, try hard to be reconciled to him on the way, or he may drag you off to the judge, and the judge turn you over to the officer, and the officer throw you into prison. I tell you, you will not get out until you have paid the last penny." NIV

Romans 13:8

Let no debt remain outstanding, except the continuing debt to love one another, for he who loves his fellowman has fulfilled the law. NIV

Diligence

Proverbs 24:30-34

I went past the field of the sluggard, past the vineyard of the man who lacks judgment; thorns had come up everywhere, the ground was covered with weeds, and the stone wall was in ruins. I applied my heart to what I observed and learned a lesson from what I saw: A little sleep, a little slumber, a little folding of the hands to rest – and poverty will come on you like a bandit and scarcity like an armed man.

*I*t is everyone's responsibility to be hard working, persistent, and diligent. The person who has no diligence is lazy – a sluggard, if you will. The sluggard. What can be said about this kind of person? Is he self-centered or lazy? Does he rest; does he do what he wants to do without regard to others? Certainly all these things probably describe a sluggard, but much more could be said.

At the very least, a sluggard has a major problem with procrastination. His motto would be to "never do today what you can put off until tomorrow"; always with good intentions; always just about ready to start a job, but not quite. The sluggard probably gets started on a few jobs, and with some of those tasks he may even get some things done, but never quite gets them finished or brought to completion.

What is his excuse? Maybe he didn't have all the tools to finish the job. Maybe he wasn't feeling well. Maybe the rain was on its way or it could be just that the sun was not shining brightly enough. Perhaps his excuse is that the job became bigger than he was expecting or it became more time consuming than he was willing to commit to. Whatever the excuse, the sluggard always finds a reason for not finishing the job.

The sluggard as portrayed in Proverbs is an example of what not to be like and presents a valuable lesson for us to learn. Proverbs 20:4 tells us that the sluggard is too lazy to pull a plow in the springtime, and therefore has no harvest in the fall. In Proverbs 22:13, he lets his mind wander, but refuses to move his body. He has always has a reason why he can't get it done.

He says there could be a lion outside, and if he goes out to work, he could be murdered in the streets! Whatever the situation, when the sluggard makes up his mind that he doesn't feel like working today, he will find an excuse to justify his inaction. He will find some kind of plausible explanation for his decision. He will leap to shirk his responsibilities, for he has a quick mind and a lazy body.

The ancient Chinese philosopher Confucius once said, "The expectations of life depend upon diligence; the mechanic that would perfect his work must first sharpen his tools."

Samuel Johnson noted, "If your determination is fixed, I do not counsel you to despair. Few things are impossible to diligence and skill. Great works are performed not by strength, but perseverance."

William Penn equates faith and diligence when he said, "Patience and diligence, like faith, remove mountains."

Proverbs 6:4

Do not give sleep to your eyes, nor slumber to your eyelids;
NASB

Proverbs 12:11, 24

He who tills his land will have plenty of bread, but he who pursues vain things lacks sense. The hand of the diligent will rule, but the slack hand will be put to forced labor. NASB

Proverbs 13:11

Wealth obtained by fraud dwindles, but the one who gathers by labor increases it. NASB

Proverbs 14:4

Where no oxen are, the manger is clean, but much increase comes by the strength of the ox. NASB

Proverbs 16:3

Commit your works to the LORD, and your plans will be established. NASB

Proverbs 21:5

The plans of the diligent lead surely to advantage, but everyone who is hasty comes surely to poverty. NASB

Proverbs 24:3-4, 7

By wisdom a house is built, and by understanding it is established; and by knowledge the rooms are filled with all precious and pleasant riches. Wisdom is too high for a fool, he does not open his mouth in the gate. NASB

Matthew 20:13

But he answered and said to one of them, 'Friend, I am doing you no wrong; did you not agree with me for a denarius? NASB

Romans 12:11

not lagging behind in diligence, fervent in spirit, serving the Lord; NASB

2 Timothy 2:6

The hard-working farmer ought to be the first to receive his share of the crops. NASB

1 Thessalonians 4:11-12

and to make it your ambition to lead a quiet life and attend to your own business and work with your hands, just as we commanded you; NASB

Dishonesty

Psalms 37:37

Mark the blameless man, and behold the upright; for the man of peace will have a posterity. NASB

Psalms 15:5

He does not put out his money at interest, nor does he take a bribe against the innocent. He who does these things will never be shaken. NASB

Psalms 62:10-12

Do not trust in oppression, and do not vainly hope in robbery; if riches increase, do not set your heart upon them. Once God has spoken; twice I have heard this: That power belongs to God; and lovingkindness is Thine, O Lord, for Thou dost recompense a man according to his work. NASB

Proverbs 10:15-16

The rich man's wealth is his fortress, the ruin of the poor is their poverty. The wages of the righteous is life, the income of the wicked, punishment. NASB

Proverbs 11:1

A false balance is an abomination to the LORD, but a just weight is His delight. A gracious woman attains honor, and violent men attain riches. The wicked earns deceptive wages, but he who sows righteousness gets a true reward. NASB

Proverbs 12:3, 12

A man will not be established by wickedness, but the root of the righteous will not be moved. The wicked desires the booty of evil men, but the root of the righteous yields fruit. NASB

Proverbs 13:7

There is one who pretends to be rich, but has nothing; another pretends to be poor, but has great wealth. Wealth obtained by fraud dwindles, but the one who gathers by labor increases it. NASB

Proverbs 15:6, 27

Much wealth is in the house of the righteous, but trouble is in the income of the wicked. He who profits illicitly troubles his own house, but he who hates bribes will live. NASB

Proverbs 16:2, 11

All the ways of a man are clean in his own sight, but the LORD weighs the motives. A just balance and scales belong to the LORD; all the weights of the bag are His concern. NASB

Proverbs 17:2

A servant who acts wisely will rule over a son who acts shamefully, and will share in the inheritance among brothers. NASB

Proverbs 20:21

An inheritance gained hurriedly at the beginning, will not be blessed in the end. NASB

Proverbs 22:28

Do not move the ancient boundary which your fathers have set. NASB

Proverbs 24:16,19-20

For a righteous man falls seven times, and rises again, but the wicked stumble in time of calamity. Do not fret because of evildoers, or be envious of the wicked; for there will be no future for the evil man; the lamp of the wicked will be put out. NASB

Proverbs 28:6

Better is the poor who walks in his integrity, than he who is crooked though he be rich. NASB

Jeremiah 9:4

Let everyone be on guard against his neighbor, and do not trust any brother; because every brother deals craftily, and every neighbor goes about as a slanderer. NASB

Matthew 18:7

Woe to the world because of its stumbling blocks! For it is inevitable that stumbling blocks come; but woe to that man through whom the stumbling block comes! NASB

Matthew 27:5

And he threw the pieces of silver into the sanctuary and departed; and he went away and hanged himself. NASB

Luke 9:25

For what is a man profited if he gains the whole world, and loses or forfeits himself? NASB

Luke 11:42

But woe to you Pharisees! For you pay tithe of mint and rue and every kind of garden herb, and yet disregard justice and the love of God; but these are the things you should have done without neglecting the others. NASB

Luke 16:1, 10-14

Jesus told his disciples: "There was a rich man whose manager was accused of wasting his possessions. "Whoever can be trusted with very little can also be trusted with much, and whoever is dishonest with very little will also be dishonest with much. So if you have not been trustworthy in handling worldly wealth, who will trust you with true riches? And if you have not been trustworthy with someone else's property, who will give you property of your own? "No servant can serve two masters. Either he will hate the one and love the other, or he will be devoted to the one and despise the other. You cannot serve both God and Money." The Pharisees, who loved money, heard all this and were sneering at Jesus. NASB

Luke 19:8

But Zacchaeus stood up and said to the Lord, "Look, Lord! Here and now I give half of my possessions to the poor, and if I have cheated anybody out of anything, I will pay back four times the amount." NASB

Luke 20:46, 47

Beware of the teachers of the law. They like to walk around in flowing robes and love to be greeted in the marketplaces and have the most important seats in the synagogues and the places of honor at banquets. They devour widows' houses and for a show make lengthy prayers. Such men will be punished most severely." NASB

Romans 2:21, 22

You, then, who teach others, do you not teach yourself? You who preach against stealing, do you steal? You who say that people should not commit adultery, do you commit adultery? You who abhor idols, do you rob temples? NASB

Envy

Psalms 73:2

But as for me, my feet had almost stumbled; my steps had nearly slipped. NKJV

Proverbs 23:17

Do not let your heart envy sinners, but be zealous for the fear of the LORD all the day; NKJV

Proverbs 24:19

Do not fret because of evildoers, nor be envious of the wicked; NKJV

Excellence

Proverbs 18:9

He who is slothful in his work is a brother to him who is a great destroyer. NKJV

Proverbs 22:29

Do you see a man who excels in his work? He will stand before kings; he will not stand before unknown men. NKJV

Colossians 3:17, 23

And whatever you do in word or deed, do all in the name of the Lord Jesus, giving thanks to God the Father through Him. And whatever you do, do it heartily, as to the Lord and not to men NKJV

1 Peter 4:11

If anyone speaks, let him speak as the oracles of God. If anyone ministers, let him do it as with the ability which God supplies, that in all things God may be glorified through Jesus Christ, to whom belong the glory and the dominion forever and ever. Amen. NKJV

Getting the Facts

Proverbs 14:8, 15

The wisdom of the prudent is to understand his way, but the folly of fools is deceit. The simple believes every word, but the prudent considers well his steps. NKJV

Proverbs 18:13

He who answers a matter before he hears it, it is folly and shame to him. NKJV

Proverbs 19:2

Also it is not good for a soul to be without knowledge, and he sins who hastens with his feet. NKJV

Proverbs 23:23

Buy the truth, and do not sell it, also wisdom and instruction and understanding. NKJV

Proverbs 27:23-24

Be diligent to know the state of your flocks, and attend to your herds; for riches are not forever, nor does a crown endure to all generations. NKJV

Luke 14:28-32

For which of you, intending to build a tower, does not sit down first and count the cost, whether he has enough to finish it — lest, after he has laid the foundation, and is not able to finish, all who see it begin to mock him, saying, 'This man began to build and was not able to finish.' Or what king, going to make war against another king, does not sit down first and consider whether he is able with ten thousand to meet him who comes against him with twenty thousand? Or else, while the other is still a great way off, he sends a delegation and asks conditions of peace. NKJV

James 1:5

If any of you lacks wisdom, let him ask of God, who gives to all liberally and without reproach, and it will be given to him. NKJV

Giving

Giving to others brings indescribable pleasure. An inward joy comes to you when you have reached out and helped others. Whether it be in monetary gifts or simply rolling up your sleeves and helping out the old-fashioned way, the act of giving brings its own reward. When you give first, your own personal needs will be automatically taken care of. After all, giving is the Lord's work. It is Christianity in action. Jesus Christ had something to say about giving to others.

Matthew 25:35-40

'For I was hungry and you gave me something to eat, I was thirsty and you gave me something to drink, I was a stranger and you invited me in, I needed clothes and you clothed me, I was sick and you looked after me, I was in prison and you came to visit me.' Then the righteous will answer him, 'Lord, when did we see you hungry and feed you, or thirsty and give you something to drink? When did we see you a stranger and invite you in, or needing clothes and clothe you? When did we see you sick or in prison and go to visit you?' The King will reply, 'I tell you the truth, whatever you did for one of the least of these brothers of mine, you did for me.'

In the verses, Jesus was not just speaking about seasonal giving. Of course, during the holiday season of Thanksgiving and Christmas many of us tend to think more often about giving to others. Some people think of giving only around these holidays. It is pleasant to give gifts to children and family, but how much more desirable is it to give gifts to someone who cannot return the favor, to someone who is not expecting anything from you? What about your giving the other 11 months of the year? How can you be a giver during that time?

Many scriptures in the Bible talk about giving. They instruct us how to give, when to give, where to give, why we give and what to give. All these verses are not meant to bring us down, point a finger in our face and discourage us. They are there to bring us happiness, merriment and a sense of well being! It is wonderful to be a giver in every sense of the word! The unhappy people in life are those who keep everything for themselves. They are the discontented ones who are selfish, living life only to please themselves and chase after their own personal wants.

Giving is fun! Giving is exciting! Just try to give something away without feeling wonderful. The non-giver is a very miserable individual. When you are feeling blue and discouraged, try giving of yourself to others. Give away something and discover what you receive in return. You will receive happiness, hope, a sense of peace and well being, and instant encouragement will come your way. Give even to your enemies. Drive them absolutely crazy with your selflessness and love.

Isaiah 66:20

And they will bring all your brothers, from all the nations, to my holy mountain in Jerusalem as an offering to the LORD — on horses, in chariots and wagons, and on mules and camels," says the LORD. "They will bring them, as the Israelites bring their grain offerings, to the temple of the LORD in ceremonially clean vessels. NIV

Psalm 96:7, 8

Ascribe to the LORD, O families of nations, ascribe to the LORD glory and strength. Ascribe to the LORD the glory due his name; bring an offering and come into his courts. NIV

Psalm 112:5

Good will come to him who is generous and lends freely, who conducts his affairs with justice. NIV

Proverbs 3:9, 10

Honor the LORD with your wealth, with the firstfruits of all your crops; then your barns will be filled to overflowing, and your vats will brim over with new wine. NIV

Proverbs 11:24-26

One man gives freely, yet gains even more; another withholds unduly, but comes to poverty. A generous man will prosper; he who refreshes others will himself be refreshed. People curse the man who hoards grain, but blessing crowns him who is willing to sell. NIV

Proverbs 28:22

A stingy man is eager to get rich and is unaware that poverty awaits him. NIV

Mark 4:24

Consider carefully what you hear," he continued. "With the measure you use, it will be measured to you-and even more. NIV

Mark 12:41-44

Jesus sat down opposite the place where the offerings were put and watched the crowd putting their money into the temple treasury. Many rich people threw in large amounts. But a poor widow came and put in two very small copper coins, worth only a fraction of a penny. Calling his disciples to him, Jesus said, "I tell you the truth, this poor widow has put more into the treasury than all the others. They all gave out of their wealth; but she, out of her poverty, put in everything-all she had to live on." NIV

Luke 6:38

Give, and it will be given to you. A good measure, pressed down, shaken together and running over, will be poured into your lap. For with the measure you use, it will be measured to you." NIV

Acts 2:45

Selling their possessions and goods, they gave to anyone as he had need. NIV

1 Corinthians 16:1, 2

Now about the collection for God's people: Do what I told the Galatian churches to do. On the first day of every week, each one of you should set aside a sum of money in keeping with his income, saving it up, so that when I come no collections will have to be made. NIV

Greed

Luke 12:16-19

The ground of a certain rich man produced a good crop. He thought to himself, 'What shall I do? I have no place to store my crops.' Then he said, 'This is what I'll do. I will tear down my barns and build bigger ones, and there I will store all my grain and my goods.

We live in an age of self-indulgence. Is it different than any previous age or just the same self-serving pleasure in a different culture? This Scripture covers the subject well, so it is probably the latter. Here we have the story of a prominent businessperson who was not satisfied with what he had. Is this bad? Not necessarily. It is proper for a businessperson to grow the business and expand the facilities and capacity of the company. It may mean new factory space to make room for new manufactured products. Maybe it is new warehouse space to house additional inventory. It might mean an expansion of current office space to be able to process new customers and a sales/service force. All of this is quite normal for a forward thinking successful enterprise. God honors forward thinking, preplanning, productivity and personal diligence.

So what about this certain rich man? What was his problem? Everything appears normal at first glance. But there was something deep inside that was not apparent perhaps to business associates, friends and neighbors. While appearing very successful on the outside, the inside rang hollow. Apparently he had planned for the present but gave no thought to planning for his future. He had not prepared for his afterlife. All of the temporary preplanning was going on, but the most important decision in his life, that of the life to come, had not been made. The clarification came as Jesus said that one who stores up material wealth without storing up spiritual riches as well, is just plain misdirected, misguided and foolish.

I Timothy 6:10 says this. "For the love of money is a root of all kinds of evil. Some people, eager for money, have wandered from the faith and pierced themselves with many griefs."

It's okay to build your friendships, have a career, become successful, grow a business, prepare for retirement, accumulate wealth and so on. But in the process of looking out for yourself, don't neglect the spiritual man. Don't forget why God desires to bless you. Prepare yourself to be a blessing to others....in this life.

Psalm 73:2, 3, 17, 20

But as for me, my feet had almost slipped; I had nearly lost my foothold. For I envied the arrogant when I saw the prosperity of the wicked. till I entered the sanctuary of God; then I understood their final destiny. As a dream when one awakes, so when you arise, O Lord, you will despise them as fantasies. NIV

Proverbs 23:4, 5

Do not wear yourself out to get rich; have the wisdom to show restraint. Cast but a glance at riches, and they are gone, for they will surely sprout wings and fly off to the sky like an eagle. NIV

Proverbs 28:25

A greedy man stirs up dissension, but he who trusts in the LORD will prosper. NIV

Luke 12:15

Then he said to them, "Watch out! Be on your guard against all kinds of greed; a man's life does not consist in the abundance of his possessions." NIV

Luke 18:24

Jesus looked at him and said, "How hard it is for the rich to enter the kingdom of God! NIV

Ephesians 5:5

For of this you can be sure: No immoral, impure or greedy person-such a man is an idolater-has any inheritance in the kingdom of Christ and of God. NIV

Helping the Less Fortunate

A 19th-century folktale is set in a small town in Russia, where a terrible cold wave was causing extreme suffering to the poor. On one bitingly cold day, the rabbi went to solicit the only wealthy man in town, a man known to be a miser.

The rabbi knocked, and the man opened the door. "Come in, Rabbi," the rich man said. Unlike everyone else in town, he was only in shirtsleeves; after all, his house was well heated. "No," the rabbi said. "No need for me to come in. I'll just be a minute." The rabbi then proceeded to engage the rich man in a lengthy conversation, asking him detailed questions concerning each member of his family. The man was shivering, yet every time he asked the rabbi to come inside, the rabbi refused.

"And your wife's cousin, the lumber merchant, how is he?" the rabbi asked. The rich man's cheeks were fiery red. "What did you come here for, Rabbi?"

"Oh, that," the rabbi said. "I need money from you to buy coal for the poor people in town." "So why don't you come in and we'll talk about it?" "Because if I come in, we will sit down by your fireplace. You will be very warm and comfortable, and when I tell you how the poor are suffering from the cold, you really won't understand. You'll give me five rubles, maybe ten, and send me away. But now, out here," the rabbi went on, indicating the frozen moisture on the man's cheeks, "when I tell you how the poor are suffering from the cold, I think you'll understand better. Right?" The man was happy to give the rabbi 100 rubles just so he could shut the door and return to his fireplace. (Jewish Humor, William Morrow & Co. Taken from Bits & Pieces, Fairfield, NJ: The Economics Press, Inc., Nov. 2000, p. 20)

Psalm 69:33

The LORD hears the needy and does not despise his captive people. NIV

Psalm 72:1, 4-15, 17

Of Solomon. Endow the king with your justice, O God, the royal son with your righteousness. He will defend the afflicted among the people and save the children of the needy; he will crush the oppressor. He will endure as long as the sun, as long as the moon, through all generations. He will be like rain falling on a mown field, like showers watering the earth. In his days the righteous will flourish; prosperity will abound till the moon is no more. He will rule from sea to sea and from the River to the ends of the earth. The desert tribes will bow before him and his enemies will lick the dust. The kings of Tarshish and of distant shores will bring tribute to him; the kings of Sheba and Seba will present him gifts. All kings will bow down to him and all nations will serve him. For he will deliver the needy who cry out, the afflicted who have no one to help. He will take pity on the weak and the needy and save the needy from death. He will rescue them from oppression and violence, for precious is their blood in his sight. Long may he live! May gold from Sheba be given him. May people ever pray for him and bless him all day long. May his name endure forever; may it continue as long as the sun. All nations will be blessed through him, and they will call him blessed. NIV

Psalm 109:31

For he stands at the right hand of the needy one, to save his life from those who condemn him. NIV

Proverbs 14:21

He who despises his neighbor sins, but blessed is he who is kind to the needy. NIV

Proverbs 14:31

He who oppresses the poor shows contempt for their Maker, but whoever is kind to the needy honors God. NIV

Matthew 5:42

Give to the one who asks you, and do not turn away from the one who wants to borrow from you. NIV

Matthew 6:19, 20

Do not store up for yourselves treasures on earth, where moth and rust destroy, and where thieves break in and steal. But store up for yourselves treasures in heaven, where moth and rust do not destroy, and where thieves do not break in and steal. NIV

Matthew 10:42

And if anyone gives even a cup of cold water to one of these little ones because he is my disciple, I tell you the truth, he will certainly not lose his reward." NIV

Luke 3:11

John answered, "The man with two tunics should share with him who has none, and the one who has food should do the same." NIV

Luke 9:48

Then he said to them, "Whoever welcomes this little child in my name welcomes me; and whoever welcomes me welcomes the one who sent me. For he who is least among you all-he is the greatest." NIV

Luke 10:35

The next day he took out two silver coins and gave them to the innkeeper. 'Look after him,' he said, 'and when I return, I will reimburse you for any extra expense you may have.' NIV

Luke 12:33

Sell your possessions and give to the poor. Provide purses for yourselves that will not wear out, a treasure in heaven that will not be exhausted, where no thief comes near and no moth destroys. NIV

Luke 19:8, 9

But Zacchaeus stood up and said to the Lord, "Look, Lord! Here and now I give half of my possessions to the poor, and if I have cheated anybody out of anything, I will pay back four times the amount." Jesus said to him, "Today salvation has come to this house, because this man, too, is a son of Abraham. NIV

1 Timothy 5:3, 8, 15, 16

Give proper recognition to those widows who are really in need. If anyone does not provide for his relatives, and especially for his immediate family, he has denied the faith and is worse than an unbeliever. Some have in fact already turned away to follow Satan. If any woman who is a believer has widows in her family, she should help them and not let the church be burdened with them, so that the church can help those widows who are really in need. NIV

I John 3:17

But whoso hath this world's good, and seethe his brother have need, and shutteth up his bowels of compassion from him, how dwelleth the love of God in him. (KJV)

1 John 3:17

If anyone has material possessions and sees his brother in need but has no pity on him, how can the love of God be in him? NIV

Hoarding & Greed

*E*cclesiastes 5:10-17 speaks to human nature and how careful we must be not to be one who is consumed with the love of money.

"He who loves money shall never have enough. The foolishness of thinking that wealth brings happiness! The more you have, the more you spend, right up to the limits of your income. So what is the advantage of wealth-except perhaps to watch it as it runs through your fingers! The man who works hard sleeps well whether he eats little or much, but the rich must worry and suffer insomnia.

There is another serious problem I have seen everywhere-savings are put into risky investments that turn sour, and soon there is nothing left to pass on to one's son. The man who speculates is soon back to where he began-with nothing. This, as I said, is a very serious problem, for all his hard work has been for nothing; he has been working for the wind. It is all swept away. All the rest of his life he is under a cloud-gloomy, discouraged, frustrated, and angry." (TLV)

Psalms 49:11,16-17

The grave is their eternal home, where they will stay forever. They may name their estates after themselves, but they leave their wealth to others. So don't be dismayed when the wicked grow rich, and their homes become ever more splendid. For when they die, they carry nothing with them. Their wealth will not follow them into the grave. NLT

Proverbs 13:22

Good people leave an inheritance to their grandchildren, but the sinner's wealth passes to the godly. NLT

Proverbs 28:22

A greedy person tries to get rich quick, but it only leads to poverty. NLT

Malachi 1:7, 9

You have despised my name by offering defiled sacrifices on my altar. Then you ask, 'How have we defiled the sacrifices?' You defile them by saying the altar of the LORD deserves no respect. Go ahead, beg God to be merciful to you! But when you bring that kind of offering, why should he show you any favor at all?" asks the LORD Almighty. NLT

Malachi 3:8

Should people cheat God? Yet you have cheated me! But you ask, 'What do you mean? When did we ever cheat you?' You have cheated me of the tithes and offerings due to me. NLT

Matthew 6:24

No one can serve two masters. For you will hate one and love the other, or be devoted to one and despise the other. You cannot serve both God and money. NLT

Matthew 19:23

Then Jesus said to his disciples, "I tell you the truth, it is very hard for a rich person to get into the Kingdom of Heaven. NLT

Luke 12:16-20

And he gave an illustration: "A rich man had a fertile farm that produced fine crops. In fact, his barns were full to overflowing. So he said, 'I know! I'll tear down my barns and build bigger ones. Then I'll have room enough to store everything. And I'll sit back and say to myself, My friend, you have enough stored away for years to come. Now take it easy! Eat, drink, and be merry!' "But God said to him, 'You fool! You will die this very night. Then who will get it all?' NLT

Luke 12:21

Yes, a person is a fool to store up earthly wealth but not have a rich relationship with God. Sell what you have and give to those in need. This will store up treasure for you in heaven! And the purses of heaven have no holes in them. Your treasure will be safe — no thief can steal it and no moth can destroy it. NLT

Honesty

Deuteronomy 25:14-15

And you must use full and honest measures. Yes, use honest weights and measures, so that you will enjoy a long life in the land the LORD your God is giving you. NLT

Psalms 112:1-3, 5

Praise the LORD! Happy are those who fear the LORD. Yes, happy are those who delight in doing what he commands. Their children will be successful everywhere; an entire generation of godly people will be blessed. They themselves will be wealthy, and their good deeds will never be forgotten. All goes well for those who are generous, who lend freely and conduct their business fairly. NLT

Proverbs 10:3,9

The LORD will not let the godly starve to death, but he refuses to satisfy the craving of the wicked. People with integrity have firm footing, but those who follow crooked paths will slip and fall. NLT

Honesty

Proverbs 13:5,11,21

Those who are godly hate lies; the wicked come to shame and disgrace. Wealth from get-rich-quick schemes quickly disappears; wealth from hard work grows. Trouble chases sinners, while blessings chase the righteous! NLT

Proverbs 16:8

It is better to be poor and godly than rich and dishonest. NLT

Proverbs 20:7

The godly walk with integrity; blessed are their children after them. NLT

Proverbs 24:27

Develop your business first before building your house. NLT

Proverbs 27:1

Don't brag about tomorrow, since you don't know what the day will bring. NLT

Proverbs 28:18

The honest will be rescued from harm, but those who are crooked will be destroyed. NLT

Proverbs 30:7-8

O God, I beg two favors from you before I die. First, help me never to tell a lie. Second, give me neither poverty nor riches! Give me just enough to satisfy my needs. NLT

Honesty versus Unmerited Gain

Deuteronomy 25:15

Yes, use honest weights and measures, so that you will enjoy a long life in the land the LORD your God is giving you. NLT

Proverbs 11:1

The LORD hates cheating, but he delights in honesty. NLT

Proverbs 16:8

It is better to be poor and godly than rich and dishonest. NLT

Proverbs 22:16

A person who gets ahead by oppressing the poor or by showering gifts on the rich will end in poverty. NLT

Proverbs 28:8

A person who makes money by charging interest will lose it. It will end up in the hands of someone who is kind to the poor. NLT

Jeremiah 22:13

And the LORD says, "Destruction is certain for Jehoiakim, who builds his palace with forced labor. By not paying wages, he builds injustice into its walls and oppression into its doorframes and ceilings. NLT

Luke 16:10

Unless you are faithful in small matters, you won't be faithful in large ones. If you cheat even a little, you won't be honest with greater responsibilities. NLT

Romans 12:17

Never pay back evil for evil to anyone. Do things in such a way that everyone can see you are honorable. NLT

Humility

1 Timothy 6:17

Command those who are rich in this present world not to be arrogant nor to put their hope in wealth, which is so uncertain.

Here is a biblical principle that reminds us not think too highly of ourselves and our accomplishments. The real truth of the matter is this. All that we have, all that we are and all good that comes to us is allowed by God. If you cannot walk in humility now, what are the chances of that happening after you have been supernaturally blessed?

When we look upon the attitudes and heart of a blessed person, what will we discover? What is the heart like? What kind of attitude does one need to receive the blessing? What about the heart of a blessed person? What theme was so important to Jesus that He talked about it more than anything else? Was it heaven? Was it repentance? Was it prayer? Was it salvation? No. It was the subject of money. He knew that if He had our money, He would certainly have our hearts.

What about the attitude of a blessed person? Overall, the principal attitude must be that all money and all possessions belong to God. He trusts us with the care of these things until we prove ourselves unworthy of His trust. It is not our money, so it's not our problem to worry about it. It is our basic responsibility as good stewards to use it correctly; decisions that are the result of a proper attitude.

Proverbs 22:4

True humility and fear of the LORD lead to riches, honor, and long life. NLT

Jeremiah 9:24

Let them boast in this alone: that they truly know me and understand that I am the LORD who is just and righteous, whose love is unfailing, and that I delight in these things. I, the LORD, have spoken! NLT

Matthew 6:1-3

Take care! Don't do your good deeds publicly, to be admired, because then you will lose the reward from your Father in heaven. When you give a gift to someone in need, don't shout about it as the hypocrites do — blowing trumpets in the synagogues and streets to call attention to their acts of charity! I assure you, they have received all the reward they will ever get. But when you give to someone, don't tell your left hand what your right hand is doing. NLT

Luke 17:3

I am warning you! If another believer sins, rebuke him; then if he repents, forgive him. NLT

Luke 19:8

Meanwhile, Zacchaeus stood there and said to the Lord, "I will give half my wealth to the poor, Lord, and if I have overcharged people on their taxes, I will give them back four times as much!" NLT

1 Corinthians 1:26-31

Remember, dear brothers and sisters, that few of you were wise in the world's eyes, or powerful, or wealthy when God called you. Instead, God deliberately chose things the world considers foolish in order to shame those who think they are wise. And he chose those who are powerless to shame those who are powerful. God chose things despised by the world, things counted as nothing at all, and used them to bring to nothing what the world considers important, so that no one can ever boast in the presence of God. God alone made it possible for you to be in Christ Jesus. For our benefit God made Christ to be wisdom itself. He is the one who made us acceptable to God. He made us pure and holy, and he gave himself to purchase our freedom. As the Scriptures say, "The person who wishes to boast should boast only of what the Lord has done." NLT

Inheritance

Proverbs 13:22

Good people leave an inheritance to their grandchildren, but the sinner's wealth passes to the godly. NLT

Proverbs 17:2

A wise slave will rule over the master's shameful sons and will share their inheritance. NLT

Proverbs 20:21

An inheritance obtained early in life is not a blessing in the end. NLT

Ecclesiastes 2:18-19, 21

I am disgusted that I must leave the fruits of my hard work to others. 19 And who can tell whether my successors will be wise or foolish? And yet they will control everything I have gained by my skill and hard work. How meaningless! For though I do my work with wisdom, knowledge, and skill, I must leave everything I gain to people who haven't worked to earn it. This is not only foolish but highly unfair. NLT

Ezekiel 46:16-18

This is what the Sovereign LORD says: If the prince gives a gift of land to one of his sons, it will belong to him and his descendants forever. But if he gives a gift of land to one of his servants, the servant may keep it only until the Year of Jubilee, which comes every fiftieth year. At that time the servant will be set free, and the land will return to the prince. Only the gifts given to the prince's sons will be permanent. And the prince may never take anyone's property by force. If he gives property to his sons, it must be from his own land, for I do not want any of my people unjustly evicted from their property." NLT

Luke 15:11-31

To illustrate the point further, Jesus told them this story: "A man had two sons. The younger son told his father, 'I want my share of your estate now, instead of waiting until you die.' So his father agreed to divide his wealth between his sons. A few days later this younger son packed all his belongings and took a trip to a distant land, and there he wasted all his money on wild living. About the time his money ran out, a great famine swept over the land, and he began to starve. He persuaded a local farmer to hire him to feed his pigs. The boy became so hungry that even the pods he was feeding the pigs looked good to him. But no one gave him anything. When he finally came to his senses, he said to himself, 'At home even the hired men have food enough to spare, and here I am, dying of hunger! I will go home to my father and say, "Father, I have sinned against both heaven and you, and I am no longer worthy of being called your son. Please take me on as a hired man."' So he returned home to his father. And while he was still a long distance away, his father saw him coming. Filled with love and compassion, he ran to his son, embraced him, and kissed him. His son said to him, 'Father, I have sinned against both heaven and you, and I am no longer worthy of being called your son.' "*But his father said to the servants, 'Quick! Bring the finest robe in the house and put it on him. Get a ring for his finger, and sandals for his feet. And kill the calf we have been fattening in the pen. We must celebrate with a feast, for this son of mine was dead and has now returned to life. He was lost, but now he is found.' So the party began.* "*Meanwhile, the older son was in the fields working. When he returned home, he heard music and dancing in the house, and he asked one of the servants what was going on. 'Your brother is back,' he was told, 'and your father has killed the calf we were fattening and has prepared a great feast. We are celebrating because of his safe return.'* "*The older brother was angry and wouldn't go in. His father came out and begged him, but he replied, 'All these years I've worked hard for you and never once refused to do a single thing you told me to. And in all that time you never gave me even one young goat for a feast with my friends. Yet when this son of yours comes back after squandering your money on prostitutes, you celebrate by killing the finest calf we have.'* "*His father said to him, 'Look, dear son, you and I are very close, and everything I have is yours. NLT*

Investing

Eternal Investments

Matthew 6:19-21

> *Do not store up for yourselves treasures on earth, where moth and rust destroy, and where thieves break in and steal. But store up for yourselves treasures in heaven, where moth and rust do not destroy, and where thieves do not break in and steal. For where your treasure is, there your heart will be also.*

Most of us understand what we classify as earthly treasures. This list includes earthly possessions such as cars, boats, clothes, houses, bank accounts, jewelry, portfolios, etc. But these things have no eternal value.

In Scripture, Jesus is warning us about protecting our hearts from the love of these things, all of which can seem so real, so lasting, so concrete, but in reality can disappear so quickly. *They can literally be here today, and gone tomorrow.*

Saul, an Old Testament king was told to utterly destroy the Amalekites, his enemy. In Samuel 15, Scripture tells us that he decided to keep the spoils of war for himself. Because he disobeyed God, his kingdom was taken from him. He lost everything because he loved earthly treasures.

This story is not so different than the New Testament story of the rich young ruler. He too had many things of earthly value. Are "things" wrong? Not necessarily. But they are a great distraction to the purpose of God. Earthly treasures can disrupt kingdom business. Are there "things" that you are holding too close that could ultimately keep you from reaching your full potential in Christ? Or even worse, make you lose your soul because of their influence?

Death is the great equalizer, the constant leveler. Some of the ancient tombs discovered in the Middle East have been found packed with food and furniture, as well as slaves. Yet all of those buried remains, buried under sand for thousands of years, have done nothing for the one who spent a lifetime accumulating them.

Our stock portfolios are always in great risk to the ups and downs of the market, the wars and rumors of wars, the economy of the nation and world, and the integrity of the company management in which we invest. Our bodies and our minds, which may seem so healthy and sharp, may be wasted by disease or crushed by a mishap tomorrow.

We invest in what we care about. If we invest our money with God, we will be interested in the ministry advance of our local church and will pray for the expansion of His kingdom locally and globally.

Note, in the Matthew 6 passage, Jesus is not saying to have nothing, enjoy nothing or that possessions are a sin. Christ is saying to us to not get too tied to these things. Be a conduit, not a dam. *It is not about what we have, but what has us.* If you center your life on things, if you base your living upon possessions, you will for sure be disappointed.

Don't base your life, your future, your well being or your happiness on the things you have accumulated. Instead, be sure you lay up for yourself the real treasures, the ones that will be of eternal value.

Notice the tone of this Scripture (Matthew 6:19-21). It doesn't seem to be a suggestion, rather a definite command of sorts. It is no secret that the rich attract a lot of interested people. While he has money, everyone wants to be near him. Should his riches disappear, so will his friends. Not much different from a beautiful, talented, young actress, singer or musician. When her beauty fades, or talent diminishes, the world looks for another to admire.

In days gone by, people accumulated wealth by the garments they possessed, the fields of grain that fed their families and gold which was used to barter for other things they needed or desired. When Jesus warned of storing earthly treasures, He knew what He was talking about. When it comes to moths, expensive clothes can be destroyed very easily. Grain can be lost to fungus and insects. Thieves can quickly make your gold disappear.

Many of the homes constructed in the ancient Middle East were made with sun-baked clay or loose stones. Although adequate for housing, it presented a comparatively easy way for thieves to dig under the wall, through the wall or by other means. No possessions were safe from those that would steal.

Of course, we know that rust can destroy even the best of tools and moths also attack things we consume. Literally, rust in its destructive path, will eat into and destroy nearly everything. Rust will eventually corrode all metal, including silver and gold. Figuratively speaking, rust can be anything that destroys you and your life. In short, all your treasures, whether physical or otherwise, can be destroyed.

The possessions we accumulate in this world are temporary at best. Each of the three metaphors found in Matthew 6:19-21 tell us together that life is short and futile. Anyone of these things, when expanded to include those things that can destroy from today's culture, clearly demonstrate to us the folly of putting our trust in earthly possessions. Bad investments, or good investments pilfered away by bad management or dishonest CEO's, can make our lifetime of savings disappear overnight.

It's not that saving or storing assets is sinful in itself. Paul notes in 2 Corinthians 12:14 that parents ought to save up for their children. When increase comes our way, we should use it, not only for our needs, but also for the good of others.

Treasures on earth can become paths to building heavenly treasures if they are used and distributed for the Glory of God. Jesus understood clearly that in the consumer culture of this world, there exists a constant battle for our affections, our hearts and our souls.

> *"Our callings are not simply secular means of making money or a living, but are God's means of utilizing our gifts and interests to His glory."* – a paraphrase of Martin Luther (1483 – 1546)

> *"Alas, how many, even among those who are called believers, have plenty of all the necessities of life, and yet complain of poverty!"* – John Wesley (1703 – 1791)

> *"Money never made a man happy yet, nor will it. There is nothing in its nature to produce happiness. The more a man has, the more he wants. Instead of its filling a vacuum, it makes one. If it satisfies one want, it doubles and trebles that want another way. That was a true proverb of the wise man, rely upon it; 'Better is little with the fear of the Lord, than great treasure, and trouble therewith.'"* –Benjamin Franklin (1706 – 1790)

Psalms 62:10

Don't try to get rich by extortion or robbery. And if your wealth increases, don't make it the center of your life. NLT

Proverbs 11:24,28

It is possible to give freely and become more wealthy, but those who are stingy will lose everything. Trust in your money and down you go! But the godly flourish like leaves in spring. NLT

Proverbs 16:1-9

We can gather our thoughts, but the LORD gives the right answer. People may be pure in their own eyes, but the LORD examines their motives. Commit your work to the LORD, and then your plans will succeed. The LORD has made everything for his own purposes, even the wicked for punishment. The LORD despises pride; be assured that the proud will be punished. Unfailing love and faithfulness cover sin; evil is avoided by fear of the LORD. When the ways of people please the LORD, he makes even their enemies live at peace with them. It is better to be poor and godly than rich and dishonest. We can make our plans, but the LORD determines our steps. NLT

Proverbs 21:5

Good planning and hard work lead to prosperity, but hasty shortcuts lead to poverty. NLT

Proverbs 23:4-5

Don't weary yourself trying to get rich. Why waste your time? For riches can disappear as though they had the wings of a bird! NLT

Investments

Proverbs 21:20

The wise have wealth and luxury, but fools spend whatever they get. NLT

Proverbs 24:27

Develop your business first before building your house. NLT

Ecclesiastes 6:3

A man might have a hundred children and live to be very old. But if he finds no satisfaction in life and in the end does not even get a decent burial, I say he would have been better off born dead. NLT

Matthew 6:19-21

Don't store up treasures here on earth, where they can be eaten by moths and get rusty, and where thieves break in and steal. Store your treasures in heaven, where they will never become moth-eaten or rusty and where they will be safe from thieves. Wherever your treasure is, there your heart and thoughts will also be. NLT

Matthew 13:22

The thorny ground represents those who hear and accept the Good News, but all too quickly the message is crowded out by the cares of this life and the lure of wealth, so no crop is produced. NLT

Matthew 25:14-30,45

Again, the Kingdom of Heaven can be illustrated by the story of a man going on a trip. He called together his servants and gave them money to invest for him while he was gone. He gave five bags of gold to one, two bags of gold to another, and one bag of gold to the last — dividing it in proportion to their abilities — and then left on his trip. The servant who received the five bags of gold began immediately to invest the money and soon doubled it. The servant with two bags of gold also went right to work and doubled the money. But the servant who received the one bag of gold dug a hole in the ground and hid the master's money for safekeeping. After a long time their master returned from his trip and called them to give an account of how they had used his money. The servant to whom he had entrusted the five bags of gold said, 'Sir, you gave me five bags of gold to invest, and I have doubled the amount.' The master was full of praise. 'Well done, my good and faithful servant. You have been faithful in handling this small amount, so now I will give you many more responsibilities. Let's celebrate together!' Next came the servant who had received the two bags of gold, with the report, 'Sir, you gave me two bags of gold to invest, and I have doubled the amount.' The master said, 'Well done, my good and faithful servant. You have been faithful in handling this small amount, so now I will give you many more responsibilities. Let's celebrate together!' "*Then the servant with the one bag of gold came and said, 'Sir, I know you are a hard man, harvesting crops you didn't plant and gathering crops you didn't cultivate. I was afraid I would lose your money, so I hid it in the earth and here it is.' "But the master replied, 'You wicked and lazy servant! You think I'm a hard man, do you, harvesting crops I didn't plant and gathering crops I didn't cultivate? Well, you should at least have put my money into the bank so I could have some interest. Take the money from this servant and give it to the one with the ten bags of gold. To those who use well what they are given, even more will be given, and they will have an abundance. But from those who are unfaithful, even what little they have will be taken away. Now throw this useless servant into outer darkness, where there will be weeping and gnashing of teeth.' And he will answer, 'I assure you, when you refused to help the least of these my brothers and sisters, you were refusing to help me.' NLT*

Luke 14:28-29

But don't begin until you count the cost. For who would begin construction of a building without first getting estimates and then checking to see if there is enough money to pay the bills? Otherwise, you might complete only the foundation before running out of funds. And then how everyone would laugh at you! NLT

Luke 19:13-26

Before he left, he called together ten servants and gave them ten pounds of silver to invest for him while he was gone.

But his people hated him and sent a delegation after him to say they did not want him to be their king. "When he returned, the king called in the servants to whom he had given the money. He wanted to find out what they had done with the money and what their profits were. The first servant reported a tremendous gain — ten times as much as the original amount! 'Well done!' the king exclaimed. 'You are a trustworthy servant. You have been faithful with the little I entrusted to you, so you will be governor of ten cities as your reward.' "The next servant also reported a good gain — five times the original amount. 'Well done!' the king said. 'You can be governor over five cities.' But the third servant brought back only the original amount of money and said, 'I hid it and kept it safe. I was afraid because you are a hard man to deal with, taking what isn't yours and harvesting crops you didn't plant.' 'You wicked servant!' the king roared. 'Hard, am I? If you knew so much about me and how tough I am, why didn't you deposit the money in the bank so I could at least get some interest on it?' Then turning to the others standing nearby, the king ordered, 'Take the money from this servant, and give it to the one who earned the most.' 'But, master,' they said, 'that servant has enough already!' 'Yes,' the king replied, 'but to those who use well what they are given, even more will be given. But from those who are unfaithful, even what little they have will be taken away. NLT

2 Peter 2:20

And when people escape from the wicked ways of the world by learning about our Lord and Savior Jesus Christ and then get tangled up with sin and become its slave again, they are worse off than before. NLT

2 Peter 3:10

But the day of the Lord will come as unexpectedly as a thief. Then the heavens will pass away with a terrible noise, and everything in them will disappear in fire, and the earth and everything on it will be exposed to judgment. NLT

Laziness

Good stewardship is not merely an occupation or a profession, rather it involves being productive. In Jesus' parable of the talents in Matthew 25, the stewards reported their earnings. One servant, however, merely hid his entrustment, and earned no increase – he lost his portion. The faithful ones not only had increases but also, received more because of their faithfulness. From the very beginning, God commanded creation to be fruitful. God is energetic, creative and imaginative, and is the life giver. Stewards are also to be concerned with productivity and so cultivate God's creation to be productive.

It is wonderful to live in a productive society. Productive societies are composed of many productive individuals. When my days are full of productive tasks I enjoy life. My normal going-to-sleep activity is to close my eyes and mentally survey all the productive things I accomplished during the day. If I have had an efficient and industrious day, I fall right to sleep.

A warning about being productive is seen in Jesus' story about the unfruitful branch of His kingdom, which He says will be cut off by the husbandman (John 15:1-5). God wants to have a productive kingdom and stewards who will be faithful.

As good stewards, we are required to work hard. If you work for someone else, you need to do it with everything you have. Give more than is required; go the second mile and the third and fourth. Proverbs 6:6-11 says, "Go to the ant, you sluggard; consider its ways and be wise! It has no commander, no overseer or ruler, yet it stores its provisions in summer and gathers its food at harvest. How long will you lie there, you sluggard? When will you get up from your sleep? A little sleep, a little slumber, a little folding of the hands to rest and poverty will come on you like a bandit and scarcity like an armed man."

Check out the ant. The ant has no one to tell it what to do – no supervisor, nor overseer, and yet it is a self-starter, a self-motivator. The ant works all summer long gathering food for the harvest season. The Scripture extends a wake-up call to the sluggard hoping for some kind of response. It says to the sluggard, "have you not slept enough?" "How long can you possibly sleep?" "Do you want to go hungry, do you want to go through life looking for handouts because you have not the wherewithal to earn your own keep?"

Proverbs 6:6-11

Go to the ant, O sluggard, observe her ways and be wise, which, having no chief, officer or ruler, prepares her food in the summer, and gathers her provision in the harvest. How long will you lie down, O sluggard? When will you arise from your sleep? A little sleep, a little slumber, a little folding of the hands to rest" — and your poverty will come in like a vagabond, and your need like an armed man. NASB

Proverbs 12:24

The hand of the diligent will rule, but the slack hand will be put to forced labor. NASB

Proverbs 13:11

Wealth obtained by fraud dwindles, but the one who gathers by labor increases it. NASB

Proverbs 14:4

Where no oxen are, the manger is clean, but much increase comes by the strength of the ox. NASB

Proverbs 19:15

Laziness casts into a deep sleep, and an idle man will suffer hunger. NASB

Proverbs 21:17

He who loves pleasure will become a poor man; he who loves wine and oil will not become rich. NASB

Proverbs 22:13

The sluggard says, "There is a lion outside; I shall be slain in the streets!" NASB

Proverbs 26:13

The sluggard says, "There is a lion in the road! A lion is in the open square!" NASB

2 Thessalonians 3:6,10

Now we command you, brethren, in the name of our Lord Jesus Christ, that you keep aloof from every brother who leads an unruly life and not according to the tradition which you received from us. For even when we were with you, we used to give you this order: if anyone will not work, neither let him eat. NASB

Lending

While borrowing, or lending for that matter, is not necessarily wrong or prohibited in Scripture, it is discouraged in a number of Scriptures. When you get into trouble because of your own unwise choices and bad decisions, while God will help you find a way out, it will not be at the expense of defrauding those to whom you owe. Forgiveness is always available, but the consequences of our wrong remain.

Exodus 22:25-26

If you lend money to My people, to the poor among you, you are not to act as a creditor to him; you shall not charge him interest. If you ever take your neighbor's cloak as a pledge, you are to return it to him before the sun sets, NASB

Deuteronomy 23:19-20

You shall not charge interest to your countrymen: interest on money, food, or anything that may be loaned at interest. You may charge interest to a foreigner, but to your countryman you shall not charge interest, so that the LORD your God may bless you in all that you undertake in the land which you are about to enter to possess. NASB

Deuteronomy 24:10-11

When you make your neighbor a loan of any sort, you shall not enter his house to take his pledge. You shall remain outside, and the man to whom you make the loan shall bring the pledge out to you. NASB

Nehemiah 5:7,10

And I consulted with myself, and contended with the nobles and the rulers and said to them, "You are exacting usury, each from his brother!" Therefore, I held a great assembly against them. "And likewise I, my brothers and my servants, are lending them money and grain. Please, let us leave off this usury. NASB

Psalms 15:5

He does not put out his money at interest, nor does he take a bribe against the innocent. He who does these things will never be shaken. NASB

Psalms 37:26

All day long he is gracious and lends; and his descendants are a blessing. NASB

Proverbs 28:8

He who increases his wealth by interest and usury, gathers it for him who is gracious to the poor. NASB

Ezekiel 18:8

If he does not lend money on interest or take increase, if he keeps his hand from iniquity, and executes true justice between man and man, NASB

Luke 6:34-35

And if you lend to those from whom you expect to receive, what credit is that to you? Even sinners lend to sinners, in order to receive back the same amount. But love your enemies, and do good, and lend, expecting nothing in return; and your reward will be great, and you will be sons of the Most High; for He Himself is kind to ungrateful and evil men. NASB

Luke 7:41

A certain moneylender had two debtors: one owed five hundred denarii, and the other fifty. NASB

Needs

Psalms 37:25

I have been young, and now I am old; yet I have not seen the righteous forsaken, or his descendants begging bread. NASB

Matthew 6:8,25-33

Therefore do not be like them; for your Father knows what you need, before you ask Him. For this reason I say to you, do not be anxious for your life, as to what you shall eat, or what you shall drink; nor for your body, as to what you shall put on. Is not life more than food, and the body than clothing? Look at the birds of the air, that they do not sow, neither do they reap, nor gather into barns, and yet your heavenly Father feeds them. Are you not worth much more than they? And which of you by being anxious can add a single cubit to his life's span? And why are you anxious about clothing? Observe how the lilies of the field grow; they do not toil nor do they spin, yet I say to you that even Solomon in all his glory did not clothe himself like one of these. But if God so arrays the grass of the field, which is alive today and tomorrow is thrown into the furnace, will He not much more do so for you, O men of little faith? Do not be anxious then, saying, 'What shall we eat?' or 'What shall we drink?' or 'With what shall we clothe ourselves?' For all these things the Gentiles eagerly seek; for your heavenly Father knows that you need all these things. But seek first His kingdom and His righteousness; and all these things shall be added to you. NASB

Philippians 4:19

And my God shall supply all your needs according to His riches in glory in Christ Jesus. NASB

Planning

Like any other success in life, quality output comes from a quality plan of action. It is impossible to reach any goal without such a road map to your success. Nothing worthwhile happens by accident. It's difficult to accomplish anything important without a detailed, specific plan.

A clear, solid plan, like the blueprint for the construction of a house, can show you which steps to take. The steps, one by one, will guide you so you will not have to stop and think about each step before taking them. You'll have the benefit of systematically following ideas that you have carefully considered in advance.

Proverbs 16:1

The plans of the heart belong to man, but the answer of the tongue is from the LORD. NASB

Pride

Psalms 75:4

I said to the boastful, 'Do not deal boastfully,' and to the wicked, 'Do not lift up the horn. NKJV

Psalms 107:40

He pours contempt on princes, and causes them to wander in the wilderness where there is no way; NKJV

Proverbs 11:2

When pride comes, then comes shame; but with the humble is wisdom. NKJV

Proverbs 12:9

Better is the one who is slighted but has a servant, than he who honors himself but lacks bread. NKJV

Proverbs 15:25

The LORD will destroy the house of the proud, but He will establish the boundary of the widow. NKJV

Proverbs 16:18-19

Pride goes before destruction, and a haughty spirit before a fall. Better to be of a humble spirit with the lowly, than to divide the spoil with the proud. NKJV

Proverbs 18:12

Before destruction the heart of a man is haughty, and before honor is humility. The poor man uses entreaties, but the rich answers roughly. NKJV

Proverbs 19:1

Better is the poor who walks in his integrity than one who is perverse in his lips, and is a fool. NKJV

Proverbs 28:11

The rich man is wise in his own eyes, but the poor who has understanding searches him out. NKJV

Proverbs 29:23

A man's pride will bring him low, but the humble in spirit will retain honor. NKJV

Jeremiah 9:23

Thus says the LORD: "Let not the wise man glory in his wisdom, let not the mighty man glory in his might, nor let the rich man glory in his riches; NKJV

Jeremiah 22:21

I spoke to you in your prosperity, but you said, 'I will not hear.' This has been your manner from your youth, That you did not obey My voice. NKJV

Matthew 23:12

And whoever exalts himself will be humbled, and he who humbles himself will be exalted. NKJV

Luke 14:11

For whoever exalts himself will be humbled, and he who humbles himself will be exalted." NKJV

Philippians 2:3

Let nothing be done through selfish ambition or conceit, but in lowliness of mind let each esteem others better than himself. NKJV

1 Timothy 6:17

Command those who are rich in this present age not to be haughty, nor to trust in uncertain riches but in the living God, who gives us richly all things to enjoy. NKJV

Prosper

Proverbs 3:10

Then your barns will be filled to overflowing, and your vats will brim over with new wine.

This is a wonderful promise, the principle of overflowing barns. It is for everyone who meets the condition which precedes the agreement. The conditions to this guarantee are two-fold. First, you are to honor God with your possessions. Second, you are to give the first fruits of all of your increase. A great principle which is wrapped by a wonderful promise. Let's see what it all means.

How do we honor the Lord? Today when we honor others we may do so at banquets, special dinners in their honor; we may give them a plaque or special award for their accomplishments or we may honor a friend by sending a card and gift. Graduates are honored with public recognition and newly weds are honored with a reception. We honor God by making sure that He holds first-place in our lives. We make sure that in the giving of our time, money, trust and prayers, He knows that our hearts are set upon Him. We place Him as Lord of our life by doing so. We honor Him with hearts full of gratitude because of His abundant blessing in our life.

Genesis 24:40

But he said to me, 'The LORD, before whom I walk, will send His angel with you and prosper your way; and you shall take a wife for my son from my family and from my father's house. NKJV

Genesis 24:42

And this day I came to the well and said, 'O LORD God of my master Abraham, if you will now prosper the way in which I go, NKJV

Genesis 26:13

The man began to prosper, and continued prospering until he became very prosperous; NKJV

Genesis 39:3

And his master saw that the LORD was with him and that the LORD made all he did to prosper in his hand. NKJV

Genesis 39:23

The keeper of the prison did not look into anything that was under Joseph's authority, because the LORD was with him; and whatever he did, the LORD made it prosper. NKJV

Deuteronomy 28:29

And you shall grope at noonday, as a blind man gropes in darkness; you shall not prosper in your ways; you shall be only oppressed and plundered continually, and no one shall save you. NKJV

Deuteronomy 29:9

Therefore keep the words of this covenant, and do them, that you may prosper in all that you do. NKJV

Deuteronomy 30:5

Then the LORD your God will bring you to the land which your fathers possessed, and you shall possess it. He will prosper you and multiply you more than your fathers. NKJV

Joshua 1:7

Only be strong and very courageous, that you may observe to do according to all the law which Moses My servant commanded you; do not turn from it to the right hand or to the left, that you may prosper wherever you go. NKJV

Ruth 4:11

And all the people who were at the gate, and the elders, said, "We are witnesses. The LORD make the woman who is coming to your house like Rachel and Leah, the two who built the house of Israel; and may you prosper in Ephrathah and be famous in Bethlehem. NKJV

I Kings 2:3

And keep the charge of the LORD your God: to walk in His ways, to keep His statutes, His commandments, His judgments, and His testimonies, as it is written in the Law of Moses, that you may prosper in all that you do and wherever you turn; NKJV

I Kings 22:12

And all the prophets prophesied so, saying, "Go up to Ramoth Gilead and prosper, for the LORD will deliver it into the king's hand." NKJV

I Kings 22:15

Then he came to the king; and the king said to him, "Micaiah, shall we go to war against Ramoth Gilead, or shall we refrain?" And he answered him, "Go and prosper, for the LORD will deliver it into the hand of the king!" NKJV

1 Chronicles 22:11

Now, my son, may the LORD be with you; and may you prosper, and build the house of the LORD your God, as He has said to you. NKJV

1 Chronicles 22:13

Then you will prosper, if you take care to fulfill the statutes and judgments with which the LORD charged Moses concerning Israel. Be strong and of good courage; do not fear nor be dismayed. NKJV

2 Chronicles 13:12

Now look, God Himself is with us as our head, and His priests with sounding trumpets to sound the alarm against you. O children of Israel, do not fight against the LORD God of your fathers, for you shall not prosper!" NKJV

2 Chronicles 18:11

And all the prophets prophesied so, saying, "Go up to Ramoth Gilead and prosper, for the LORD will deliver it into the king's hand." NKJV

2 Chronicles 18:14

Then he came to the king; and the king said to him, "Micaiah, shall we go to war against Ramoth Gilead, or shall I refrain?" And he said, "Go and prosper, and they shall be delivered into your hand!" NKJV

2 Chronicles 20:20

So they rose early in the morning and went out into the Wilderness of Tekoa; and as they went out, Jehoshaphat stood and said, "Hear me, O Judah and you inhabitants of Jerusalem: Believe in the LORD your God, and you shall

be established; believe His prophets, and you shall prosper." NKJV

2 Chronicles 24:20

Then the Spirit of God came upon Zechariah the son of Jehoiada the priest, who stood above the people, and said to them, "Thus says God: 'Why do you transgress the commandments of the LORD, so that you cannot prosper? Because you have forsaken the LORD, He also has forsaken you.'" NKJV

2 Chronicles 26:5

He sought God in the days of Zechariah, who had understanding in the visions of God; and as long as he sought the LORD, God made him prosper. NKJV

2 Chronicles 31:21

And every work which he began in the service of the house of God in law and in commandment, seeking his God, he did with all his heart and prospered. NASB

Nehemiah 1:11

O Lord, I pray, please let Your ear be attentive to the prayer of Your servant, and to the prayer of Your servants who desire to fear Your name; and let Your servant prosper this day, I

pray, and grant him mercy in the sight of this man." For I was the king's cupbearer. NKJV

Nehemiah 2:20

So I answered them, and said to them, "The God of heaven Himself will prosper us; therefore we His servants will arise and build, but you have no heritage or right or memorial in Jerusalem." NKJV

Job 8:6

If you were pure and upright, surely now He would awake for you, and prosper your rightful dwelling place. NKJV

Job 12:6

6 The tents of robbers prosper, and those who provoke God are secure-- in what God provides by His hand. NKJV

Psalms 1:3

He shall be like a tree planted by the rivers of water, that brings forth its fruit in its season, whose leaf also shall not wither; and whatever he does shall prosper. NKJV

Psalms 122:6

Pray for the peace of Jerusalem: "May they prosper who love you. NKJV

Proverbs 28:13

He who covers his sins will not prosper, but whoever confesses and forsakes them will have mercy. NKJV

Ecclesiastes 11:6

In the morning sow your seed, and in the evening do not withhold your hand; for you do not know which will prosper, either this or that, or whether both alike will be good. NKJV

Isaiah 48:15

I, even I, have spoken; yes, I have called him, I have brought him, and his way will prosper. NKJV

Isaiah 53:10

Yet it pleased the LORD to bruise Him; he has put Him to grief. When You make His soul an offering for sin, he shall see His seed, He shall prolong His days, and the pleasure of the LORD shall prosper in His hand. NKJV

Isaiah 54:17

No weapon formed against you shall prosper, and every tongue which rises against you in judgment you shall condemn. This is the heritage of the servants of the LORD, and their righteousness is from Me," says the LORD. NKJV

Isaiah 55:11

So shall My word be that goes forth from My mouth; it shall not return to Me void, but it shall accomplish what I please, and it shall prosper in the thing for which I sent it. NKJV

Jeremiah 2:37

Indeed you will go forth from him with your hands on your head; for the LORD has rejected your trusted allies, and you will not prosper by them. NKJV

Jeremiah 5:28

They have grown fat, they are sleek; yes, they surpass the deeds of the wicked; they do not plead the cause, the cause of the fatherless; yet they prosper, and the right of the needy they do not defend. NKJV

Jeremiah 10:21

For the shepherds have become dull-hearted, and have not sought the LORD; therefore they shall not prosper, and all their flocks shall be scattered. NKJV

Jeremiah 12:1

Righteous are You, O LORD, when I plead with You; yet let me talk with You about Your judgments. Why does the way of the wicked prosper? Why are those happy who deal so treacherously? NKJV

Jeremiah 20:11

But the LORD is with me as a mighty, awesome One. Therefore my persecutors will stumble, and will not prevail. They will be greatly ashamed, for they will not prosper. Their everlasting confusion will never be forgotten. NKJV

Jeremiah 22:30

Thus says the LORD: 'Write this man down as childless, a man who shall not prosper in his days; for none of his descendants shall prosper, sitting on the throne of David, and ruling anymore in Judah.' NKJV

Jeremiah 23:5-6

Behold, the days are coming," says the LORD, "That I will raise to David a Branch of righteousness; a King shall reign and prosper, and execute judgment and righteousness in the earth. In His days Judah will be saved, and Israel will dwell safely; now this is His name by which He will be called: THE LORD OUR RIGHTEOUSNESS. NKJV

Lamentations 1:5

Her adversaries have become the master, her enemies prosper; for the LORD has afflicted her because of the multitude of her transgressions. Her children have gone into captivity before the enemy. NKJV

Ezekiel 17:15

'But he rebelled against him by sending his ambassadors to Egypt, that they might give him horses and many people. Will he prosper? Will he who does such things escape? Can he break a covenant and still be delivered? NKJV

Daniel 8:24

His power shall be mighty, but not by his own power; he shall destroy fearfully, and shall prosper and thrive; he shall destroy the mighty, and also the holy people. NKJV

Daniel 8:25

Through his cunning he shall cause deceit to prosper under his rule; and he shall exalt himself in his heart. He shall destroy many in their prosperity. He shall even rise against the Prince of princes; but he shall be broken without human means. NKJV

Daniel 11:27

Both these kings' hearts shall be bent on evil, and they shall speak lies at the same table; but it shall not prosper, for the end will still be at the appointed time. NKJV

Daniel 11:36

Then the king shall do according to his own will: he shall exalt and magnify himself above every god, shall speak blasphemies against the God of gods, and shall prosper till the wrath has been accomplished; for what has been determined shall be done. NKJV

1 Corinthians 16:2

On the first day of the week let each one of you lay something aside, storing up as he may prosper, that there be no collections when I come. NKJV

3 John 1:2

Beloved, I pray that you may prosper in all things and be in health, just as your soul prospers. NKJV

Prosperity

Deuteronomy 28:12

The LORD will open the heavens, the storehouse of his bounty, to send rain on your land in season and to bless all the work of your hands. You will lend to many nations but will borrow from none."

One way God opens the windows of heaven is by keeping us from untold financial disasters. Malachi 3:10-11 says, "Bring ye all the tithes into the storehouse, that there may be meat in mine house, and prove me now herewith, saith the LORD of hosts, if I will not open you the windows of heaven, and pour you out a blessing, that there shall not be room enough to receive it. And I will rebuke the devourer for your sakes, and he shall not destroy the fruits of your ground; neither shall your vine cast her fruit before the time in the field, saith the LORD of hosts" (KJV).

What does it mean to "rebuke the devourer"? Many things create havoc in our financial lives. It may be the loss of a job, auto repair expenses, house maintenance, appliance breakdown, or healthcare related expenses. From time to time we all can acknowledge some difficulty in these areas. And when "out of nowhere" expenses come alongside us, they can be burdensome and costly.

However, what we don't know is all that God keeps away from us. When we are faithful in our giving, the Word simply states that our crops will be large and that He will keep the insects and plagues away. Whether you are a farmer, a tiller of the ground, or simply planting crops of a nonagricultural nature, you can rest assured God is working on your behalf.

Yet another way God opens the windows of heaven is by blessing us when we give. Generosity is God's antidote to greed. The heart and attitude of a blessed person is worth looking at. After all, do we not all want to be a blessed person? Blessed people are set apart in many ways because they have learned how to be blessed. We all have the opportunity to receive the blessing of God and be "under the shadow of the Almighty" (Psalm 91:1) if we so desire. The blessed person gives of his / her resources freely, cheerfully, and out of genuine appreciation to God.

When we look upon the attitudes and heart of a blessed person, what will we discover? What is the heart like? What kind of attitude does one need to receive the blessing? What about the heart of a blessed person? What theme was so important to Jesus that He talked about it more than anything else? Was it heaven? Was it repentance? Was it prayer? Was it salvation? No. It was the subject of money. He knew that if He had our money, He would certainly have our hearts.

What about the attitude of a blessed person? Overall, the principal attitude must be that all money and all possessions belong to God. He trusts us with the care of these things until we prove ourselves unworthy of His trust. It is not our money, so it's not our problem to worry about it. It is our basic responsibility as good stewards to use it correctly.

Deuteronomy 23:5 -6

You shall not seek their peace nor their prosperity all your days forever. NIV

Deuteronomy 28:11

And the LORD will make you abound in prosperity, in the offspring of your body and in the offspring of your beast and in the produce of your ground, in the land which the LORD swore to your fathers to give you. NASB

1 Samuel 25:5-6

And thus you shall say to him who lives in prosperity: 'Peace be to you, peace to your house, and peace to all that you have! NIV

1 Kings 10:7

However I did not believe the words until I came and saw with my own eyes; and indeed the half was not told me. Your wisdom and prosperity exceed the fame of which I heard. NIV

Ezra 9:12-13

Now therefore, do not give your daughters as wives for their sons, nor take their daughters to your sons; and never seek their peace or prosperity, that you may be strong and eat the good of the land, and leave it as an inheritance to your children forever.' NIV

Job 15:21

Dreadful sounds are in his ears; In prosperity the destroyer comes upon him. NIV

Job 21:16

Indeed their prosperity is not in their hand; the counsel of the wicked is far from me. NIV

Job 30:15

Terrors are turned upon me; They pursue my honor as the wind, and my prosperity has passed like a cloud. NIV

Job 36:11-12

If they obey and serve Him, They shall spend their days in prosperity, And their years in pleasures. But if they do not obey, They shall perish by the sword, And they shall die without knowledge. NIV

Psalms 25:13

He himself shall dwell in prosperity, And his descendants shall inherit the earth. NIV

Psalms 30:6-7

Now in my prosperity I said, "I shall never be moved." LORD, by Your favor You have made my mountain stand strong; You hid Your face, and I was troubled. NIV

Psalms 35:27

Let them shout for joy and be glad, Who favor my righteous cause; And let them say continually, "Let the LORD be magnified, Who has pleasure in the prosperity of His servant." NIV

Psalms 68:6

God sets the solitary in families; He brings out those who are bound into prosperity; But the rebellious dwell in a dry land. NIV

Psalms 73:3

For I was envious of the boastful, When I saw the prosperity of the wicked. NIV

Psalms 118:25

Save now, I pray, O LORD; O LORD, I pray, send now prosperity. NIV

Psalms 122:7

Peace be within your walls, Prosperity within your palaces." NIV

Ecclesiastes 7:14

In the day of prosperity be joyful, But in the day of adversity consider: Surely God has appointed the one as well as the other, So that man can find out nothing that will come after him. NIV

Jeremiah 22:21

I spoke to you in your prosperity, But you said, 'I will not hear.' This has been your manner from your youth, That you did not obey My voice. NIV

Jeremiah 33:9

Then it shall be to Me a name of joy, a praise, and an honor before all nations of the earth, who shall hear all the good that I do to them; they shall fear and tremble for all the goodness and all the prosperity that I provide for it.' NIV

Lamentations 3:17-18

You have moved my soul far from peace; I have forgotten prosperity. And I said, "My strength and my hope Have perished from the LORD." NIV

Daniel 4:27

Therefore, O king, let my advice be acceptable to you; break off your sins by being righteous, and your iniquities by showing mercy to the poor. Perhaps there may be a lengthening of your prosperity." NIV

Daniel 8:25

Through his cunning He shall cause deceit to prosper under his rule; And he shall exalt himself in his heart. He shall destroy many in their prosperity. He shall even rise against the Prince of princes; But he shall be broken without human means. NIV

Zechariah 1:17

Again proclaim, saying, 'Thus says the LORD of hosts: "My cities shall again spread out through prosperity; The LORD will again comfort Zion, And will again choose Jerusalem.' NIV

Acts 19:25

He called them together with the workers of similar occupation, and said: "Men, you know that we have our prosperity by this trade. NIV

Acts 24:2-4

And when he was called upon, Tertullus began his accusation, saying: "Seeing that through you we enjoy great peace, and prosperity is being brought to this nation by your foresight, we accept it always and in all places, most noble Felix, with all thankfulness. NIV

Luke 15:13

And not many days later, the younger son gathered everything together and went on a journey into a distant country, and there he squandered his estate with loose living. NASB

John 6:12

And when they were filled, He said to His disciples, "Gather up the leftover fragments that nothing may be lost." NASB

Prosperous

Genesis 24:2

And the man, wondering at her, remained silent so as to know whether the LORD had made his journey prosperous or not. NKJV

Genesis 26:13

The man began to prosper, and continued prospering until he became very prosperous; NKJV

Genesis 30:4

Thus the man became exceedingly prosperous, and had large flocks, female and male servants, and camels and donkeys. NKJV

Joshua 1:8

This Book of the Law shall not depart from your mouth, but you shall meditate in it day and night, that you may observe to do according to all that is written in it. For then you will make your way prosperous, and then you will have good success. NKJV

Judges 18:5

So they said to him, "Please inquire of God, that we may know whether the journey on which we go will be prosperous." NKJV

Psalms 22:29

All the prosperous of the earth shall eat and worship; all those who go down to the dust shall bow before Him, even he who cannot keep himself alive. NKJV

Zechariah 7:7

Should you not have obeyed the words which the LORD proclaimed through the former prophets when Jerusalem and the cities around it were inhabited and prosperous, and the South and the Lowland were inhabited? NKJV

Zechariah 8:12

For the seed shall be prosperous, The vine shall give its fruit, The ground shall give her increase, and the heavens shall give their dew-- I will cause the remnant of this people To possess all these. NKJV

Retirement

Psalms 37:25

I have been young, and now I am old; yet I have not seen the righteous forsaken, or his descendants begging bread. NASB

Proverbs 16:31

A gray head is a crown of glory; it is found in the way of righteousness. NASB

Proverbs 20:29

The glory of young men is their strength, and the honor of old men is their gray hair. NASB

Rich & Riches

1 Timothy 6:7

For we brought nothing into the world, and we can take nothing out of it.

It's pretty tough to read this Scripture and come away with any other thought. It is simple, yet profound. Short yet meaningful. We all should remind ourselves of this every day. The following is a very meaningful story which was written by Dr. Billy Graham.

> "A little child was playing one day with a very valuable vase. He put his hand into it and could not withdraw it. His father too, tried his best, but all in vain. They were thinking of breaking the vase when the father said, 'Now, my son, make one more try. Open your hand and hold your fingers out straight as you see me doing, and then pull.' To their astonishment the little fellow said, "Oh no, father. I couldn't put my fingers out like that, because if I did I would drop my penny." Smile, if you will--but thousands of us are like that little boy, so busy holding on to the world's worthless penny that we cannot accept liberation. I beg you to drop the trifle in your heart. Surrender! Let go!"

Genesis 13:2

Abram was very rich in livestock, in silver, and in gold. NKJV

Genesis 14:23

That I will take nothing, from a thread to a sandal strap, and that I will not take anything that is yours, lest you should say, 'I have made Abram rich'-- NKJV

Genesis 49:20

Bread from Asher shall be rich, and he shall yield royal dainties. NKJV

Exodus 30:15

The rich shall not give more and the poor shall not give less than half a shekel, when you give an offering to the LORD, to make atonement for yourselves. NKJV

Leviticus 25:47

Now if a sojourner or stranger close to you becomes rich, and one of your brethren who dwells by him becomes poor, and sells himself to the stranger or sojourner close to you, or to a member of the stranger's family, NKJV

Numbers 13:20

Whether the land is rich or poor; and whether there are forests there or not. Be of good courage. And bring some of the fruit of the land." Now the time was the season of the first ripe grapes. NKJV

Ruth 3:10

Then he said, "Blessed are you of the LORD, my daughter! For you have shown more kindness at the end than at the beginning, in that you did not go after young men, whether poor or rich. NKJV

1 Samuel 2:7

The LORD makes poor and makes rich; He brings low and lifts up. NKJV

1 Samuel 25:2

Now there was a man in Maon whose business was in Carmel, and the man was very rich. He had three thousand sheep and a thousand goats. And he was shearing his sheep in Carmel. NKJV

2 Samuel 12:1

Then the LORD sent Nathan to David. And he came to him, and said to him: "There were two men in one city, one rich and the other poor. NKJV

2 Samuel 12:2

The rich man had exceedingly many flocks and herds. NKJV

2 Samuel 12:4

And a traveler came to the rich man, who refused to take from his own flock and from his own herd to prepare one for the wayfaring man who had come to him; but he took the poor man's lamb and prepared it for the man who had come to him. NKJV

2 Samuel 19:32

Now Barzillai was a very aged man, eighty years old. And he had provided the king with supplies while he stayed at Mahanaim, for he was a very rich man. NKJV

1 Chronicles 4:40

And they found rich, good pasture, and the land was broad, quiet, and peaceful; for some Hamites formerly lived there. NKJV

Nehemiah 9:25

And they took strong cities and a rich land, and possessed houses full of all goods, cisterns already dug, vineyards, olive groves, and fruit trees in abundance. So they ate and were filled and grew fat, and delighted themselves in your great goodness. NKJV

Nehemiah 9:35

For they have not served You in their kingdom, or in the many good things that you gave them, or in the large and rich land which You set before them; nor did they turn from their wicked works. NKJV

Job 15:29

He will not be rich, nor will his wealth continue, nor will his possessions overspread the earth. NKJV

Job 27:19

He rich man will lie down, but not be gathered up; he opens his eyes, and he is no more. NKJV

Job 34:19

Yet He is not partial to princes, nor does He regard the rich more than the poor; for they are all the work of His hands. NKJV

Psalms 45:12

And the daughter of Tyre will come with a gift; the rich among the people will seek your favor. NKJV

Psalms 49:2

Both low and high, rich and poor together. NKJV

Psalms 49:16

Do not be afraid when one becomes rich, when the glory of his house is increased; NKJV

Psalms 66:12

You have caused men to ride over our heads; we went through fire and through water; but You brought us out to rich fulfillment. NKJV

Proverbs 10:4

He who has a slack hand becomes poor, but the hand of the diligent makes rich. NKJV

Proverbs 10:15

The rich man's wealth is his strong city; the destruction of the poor is their poverty. NKJV

Proverbs 10:22

The blessing of the LORD makes one rich, and He adds no sorrow with it. NKJV

Proverbs 11:25

The generous soul will be made rich, and he who waters will also be watered himself. NKJV

Proverbs 13:4

The soul of a lazy man desires, and has nothing; but the soul of the diligent shall be made rich. NKJV

Proverbs 13:7

There is one who makes himself rich, yet has nothing; and one who makes himself poor, yet has great riches. NKJV

Proverbs 14:20

The poor man is hated even by his own neighbor, but the rich has many friends. NKJV

Proverbs 18:11

The rich man's wealth is his strong city, and like a high wall in his own esteem. NKJV

Proverbs 18:23

The poor man uses entreaties, but the rich answers roughly. NKJV

Proverbs 21:17

He who loves pleasure will be a poor man; he who loves wine and oil will not be rich. NKJV

Proverbs 22:2

The rich and the poor have this in common, the LORD is the maker of them all. NKJV

Proverbs 22:7

The rich rules over the poor, and the borrower is servant to the lender. NKJV

Proverbs 22:16

He who oppresses the poor to increase his riches, and he who gives to the rich, will surely come to poverty. NKJV

Colosians1:27

To them God willed to make known what are the riches of the glory of this mystery among the Gentiles: which is Christ in you, the hope of glory. NKJV

Colossians 2:2

That their hearts may be encouraged, being knit together in love, and attaining to all riches of the full assurance of understanding, to the knowledge of the mystery of God, both of the Father and of Christ, NKJV

1 Timothy 6:17

Command those who are rich in this present age not to be haughty, nor to trust in uncertain riches but in the living God, who gives us richly all things to enjoy. NKJV

Hebrews 11:26

Esteeming the reproach of Christ greater riches than the treasures in Egypt; for he looked to the reward. NKJV

James 5:2

Your riches are corrupted, and your garments are moth-eaten. NKJV

Revelation 5:12

Saying with a loud voice: "Worthy is the Lamb who was slain To receive power and riches and wisdom, And strength and honor and glory and blessing!" NKJV

Revelation 18:17

For in one hour such great riches came to nothing.' Every shipmaster, all who travel by ship, sailors, and as many as trade on the sea, stood at a distance. NKJV)

Saving

The secret of financial success is to spend what you have left after saving, instead of saving what is left after spending.

Saving money is hard work. And the hardest part is simply getting started. If you're beginning from scratch, consider this three-part strategy:

1. Save for the unexpected—three to six month's worth of living expenses. In case you lose a job or find yourself with no steady income, this rainy-day fund will become necessary. Take no chances with this money. Keep it readily available, in a bank account or a money-market mutual fund.

2. Save for long-range expenses—a new home or college for the kids. Be more flexible with this money. Keep it in long-term certificates of deposit or in Series EE Savings Bonds. You'll earn more interest than in a conventional bank account and you can time your investment so the money is available when you need it.

3. Save for retirement. That can mean an Individual Retirement Account, a company retirement plan, or other solid financial investments. A conservative mutual fund that invests only in top-quality stocks is one possibility. Or you might risk a little more for a greater reward by investing in a mutual fund that buys growth stocks.

Proverbs 6:6-8

Go to the ant, O sluggard, observe her ways and be wise, which, having no chief, Officer or ruler, prepares her food in the summer, and gathers her provision in the harvest. NASB

Proverbs 21:20

There is precious treasure and oil in the dwelling of the wise, but a foolish man swallows it up. NASB

Proverbs 30:24-25

Four things are small on the earth, but they are exceedingly wise: The ants are not a strong folk, but they prepare their food in the summer; NASB

Self-Control

*I*f a person or family will live a restrained lifestyle, they will be able to live on thousands of dollars less each year. You should only incur debt when it makes good economic sense. The expense of borrowing should be less than the economic benefit that you will receive.

Don't underestimate God's desire to help you in every way. Over and over the Scriptures indicate that you are to live a controlled and temperate lifestyle.

> "Now the overseer must be above reproach..... temperate, self-controlled, respectable...." (I Timothy 3:2 NIV).

Matthew 7:13, 14

> *Enter through the narrow gate. For wide is the gate and broad is the road that leads to destruction, and many enter through it. But small is the gate and narrow the road that leads to life, and only a few find it.* NIV

2 Corinthians 8:11

> *Now finish the work, so that your eager willingness to do it may be matched by your completion of it, according to your means.* NIV

2 Thessalonians 3:11

We hear that some among you are idle. They are not busy; they are busybodies. NIV

Hebrews 12:11

No discipline seems pleasant at the time, but painful. Later on, however, it produces a harvest of righteousness and peace for those who have been trained by it. NIV

Sharing

Proverbs 19:17

He who is kind to the poor lends to the LORD, and he will reward him for what he has done.

In America, and many other nations all around the world, this generation has access to untold quantities of wealth. Yet even though our wealth and blessing has increased, still the need to give money to the poor, and food to the hungry, has never been greater than right now. Untold millions are needed to reach the world with the Gospel. Our first priority is to read, know and obey the Word of God.

The following story is told/written by Louis Lehman in the March 1999 edition of Guideposts.

> "When I was growing up, my father used to say, 'No matter who they are or what they do, treat your neighbors with love.' I didn't fully understand what he meant until on Sunday on our way to church, when we spotted someone shoveling corn from our crib into a battered old truck. Dad stopped the car and got out. The man looked up and froze. I knew this man. Everybody in town suspected him of stealing their gas! No one had ever confronted him for fear of his violent temper. Now we'd caught him red-handed. What was Dad going to do? "If that's not enough," my father said evenly "come back tomorrow. Take as much as you need. Remember, you're my neighbor." The man dropped his shovel and hung his head.

He never stole from us or anyone else in town again, as far as I know. Perhaps he learned how to be a good neighbor that day. I know I did."

How would you have reacted? What would you have done if someone in need stole from you? If we are kind to the poor the Scripture promises us that in doing so we are lending to the Lord. Lending to the Lord brings great reward both in this life and the life to come.

Exodus 16:18-20

And when they measured it by the omer, he who gathered much did not have too much, and he who gathered little did not have too little. Each one gathered as much as he needed. Then Moses said to them, "No one is to keep any of it until morning." However, some of them paid no attention to Moses; they kept part of it until morning, but it was full of maggots and began to smell. So Moses was angry with them. NIV

Acts 4:32

All the believers were one in heart and mind. No one claimed that any of his possessions was his own, but they shared everything they had. NIV

Romans 12:13

Share with God's people who are in need. Practice hospitality. NIV

1 Corinthians 9:7-11, 14

*Who serves as a soldier at his own expense? Who plants a vineyard and does not eat of its grapes? Who tends a flock and does not drink of the milk? Do I say this merely from a human point of view? Doesn't the Law say the same thing? For it is written in the Law of Moses: "Do not muzzle an ox while it is treading out the grain." Is it about oxen that God is concerned? Surely he says this for us, doesn't he? Yes, this was written for us, because when the plowman plows and the thresher threshes, they ought to do so in the hope of sharing in the harvest. If we have sown spiritual seed among you, is it too much if we reap a material harvest from you? In the same way, the Lord has commanded that those who preach the gospel should receive their living from the gospel.
NIV*

2 Corinthians 8:8-15

I am not commanding you, but I want to test the sincerity of your love by comparing it with the earnestness of others. For you know the grace of our Lord Jesus Christ, that though he was rich, yet for your sakes he became poor, so that you through his poverty might become rich. And here is my advice about what is best for you in this matter: Last year you were the first not only to give but also to have the desire to do so. Now finish the work, so that your eager willingness to do it may be matched by your completion of it, according to your means. For if the willingness is there, the gift is acceptable according to what one has, not according to what he does not have. Our desire is not that others might be relieved while you are hard pressed, but that there might be equality. At the present time your plenty will supply what they need, so that in turn their plenty will supply what you need. Then there will be equality, as it is written: "He who gathered much did not have too much, and he who gathered little did not have too little. NIV

2 Corinthians 9:6-13

Remember this: Whoever sows sparingly will also reap sparingly, and whoever sows generously will also reap generously. Each man should give what he has decided in his heart to give, not reluctantly or under compulsion, for God loves a cheerful giver. And God is able to make all grace abound to you, so that in all things at all times, having all that you need, you will abound in every good work. As it is written: "He has scattered abroad his gifts to the poor; his righteousness endures forever." Now he who supplies seed to the sower and bread for food will also supply and increase your store of seed and will enlarge the harvest of your righteousness. You will be made rich in every way so that you can be generous on every occasion, and through us your generosity will result in thanksgiving to God. This service that you perform is not only supplying the needs of God's people but is also overflowing in many expressions of thanks to God. Because of the service by which you have proved yourselves, men will praise God for the obedience that accompanies your confession of the gospel of Christ, and for your generosity in sharing with them and with everyone else. NIV

Galatians 6:6

Anyone who receives instruction in the word must share all good things with his instructor. NIV

Slothfulness

Proverbs 18:9

One who is slack in his work is brother to one who destroys. NIV

Proverbs 24:30, 31

I went past the field of the sluggard, past the vineyard of the man who lacks judgment; thorns had come up everywhere, the ground was covered with weeds, and the stone wall was in ruins. NIV

Ecclesiastes 10:18

If a man is lazy, the rafters sag; if his hands are idle, the house leaks. NIV

2 Thessalonians 3:11

We hear that some among you are idle. They are not busy; they are busybodies. NIV

Hebrews 6:12

We do not want you to become lazy, but to imitate those who through faith and patience inherit what has been promised. NIV

Speculation

Ecclesiastes 5:15-17

Naked a man comes from his mother's womb, and as he comes, so he departs. He takes nothing from his labor that he can carry in his hand. This too is a grievous evil: As a man comes, so he departs, and what does he gain, since he toils for the wind? All his days he eats in darkness, with great frustration, affliction and anger. NIV

Suing

Matthew 5:42

Give to the one who asks you, and do not turn away from the one who wants to borrow from you. NIV

Matthew 6:3

But when you give to the needy, do not let your left hand know what your right hand is doing, NIV

Matthew 10:42

And if anyone gives even a cup of cold water to one of these little ones because he is my disciple, I tell you the truth, he will certainly not lose his reward." NIV

Matthew 13:12

Whoever has will be given more, and he will have an abundance. Whoever does not have, even what he has will be taken from him. NIV

Luke 6:30-36

Give to everyone who asks you, and if anyone takes what belongs to you, do not demand it back. Do to others as you would have them do to you. "If you love those who love you, what credit is that to you? Even 'sinners' love those who love them. And if you do good to those who are good to you, what credit is that to you? Even 'sinners' do that. And if you lend to those from whom you expect repayment, what credit is that to you? Even 'sinners' lend to 'sinners,' expecting to be repaid in full. But love your enemies, do good to them, and lend to them without expecting to get anything back. Then your reward will be great, and you will be sons of the Most High, because he is kind to the ungrateful and wicked. Be merciful, just as your Father is merciful. NIV

Luke 12:57, 58

Why don't you judge for yourselves what is right? As you are going with your adversary to the magistrate, try hard to be reconciled to him on the way, or he may drag you off to the judge, and the judge turn you over to the officer, and the officer throw you into prison. NIV

1 Corinthians 6:1-7

If any of you has a dispute with another, dare he take it before the ungodly for judgment instead of before the saints? Do you not know that the saints will judge the world? And if you are to judge the world, are you not competent to judge trivial cases? Do you not know that we will judge angels? How much more the things of this life! Therefore, if you have disputes about such matters, appoint as judges even men of little account in the church! I say this to shame you. Is it possible that there is nobody among you wise enough to judge a dispute between believers? But instead, one brother goes to law against another-and this in front of unbelievers!

The very fact that you have lawsuits among you means you have been completely defeated already. Why not rather be wronged? Why not rather be cheated? NIV

Supporting the Wealthy

Deuteronomy 1:17

Do not show partiality in judging; hear both small and great alike. Do not be afraid of any man, for judgment belongs to God. Bring me any case too hard for you, and I will hear it. NIV

Deuteronomy 16:19

Do not pervert justice or show partiality. Do not accept a bribe, for a bribe blinds the eyes of the wise and twists the words of the righteous. NIV

Proverbs 14:20

But any winged creature that is clean you may eat. NIV

Proverbs 28:21

To show partiality is not good — yet a man will do wrong for a piece of bread. NIV

Taxes

Matthew 17:24-27

After Jesus and his disciples arrived in Capernaum, the collectors of the two-drachma tax came to Peter and asked, "Doesn't your teacher pay the temple tax?" "Yes, he does," he replied. When Peter came into the house, Jesus was the first to speak. "What do you think, Simon?" he asked. "From whom do the kings of the earth collect duty and taxes-from their own sons or from others?" "From others," Peter answered. "Then the sons are exempt," Jesus said to him. "But so that we may not offend them, go to the lake and throw out your line. Take the first fish you catch; open its mouth and you will find a four-drachma coin. Take it and give it to them for my tax and yours." NIV

Mark 12:14-17

They came to him and said, "Teacher, we know you are a man of integrity. You aren't swayed by men, because you pay no attention to who they are; but you teach the way of God in accordance with the truth. Is it right to pay taxes to Caesar or not? Should we pay or shouldn't we?" But Jesus knew their hypocrisy. "Why are you trying to trap me?" he asked. "Bring me a denarius and let me look at it." They brought the coin, and he asked them, "Whose portrait is this? And whose inscription?" "Caesar's," they replied. Then Jesus said to them, "Give to Caesar what is Caesar's and to God what is God's." And they were amazed at him. NIV

Luke 20:22-25

Is it right for us to pay taxes to Caesar or not?" He saw through their duplicity and said to them, "Show me a denarius. Whose portrait and inscription are on it?" "Caesar's," they replied. He said to them, "Then give to Caesar what is Caesar's, and to God what is God's." NIV

Romans 13:6, 7

This is also why you pay taxes, for the authorities are God's servants, who give their full time to governing. Give everyone what you owe him: If you owe taxes, pay taxes; if revenue, then revenue; if respect, then respect; if honor, then honor. NIV

Tithing

The tithe is the first part of our income. It is to be set apart before the rent, before the bills and before we go shopping because it belongs to God and He must come first in our lives. We are to give it to the Lord as a token of gratefulness, recognizing that the Lord is the originator of ALL our income.

The "tithe" simply means the "tenth." A "tenth" is 10%. A ratio of 1 to 10 is easy to remember and easy to figure; much like our decimal system today. It seems natural and logical to divide things into tens.

- Tithing is scriptural.
- Tithing is systematic.
- Tithing is simple.
- Tithing is successful.
- Tithing is right.

God has ordained that the use of money is related to spiritual values. The only way to get our treasures into heaven is to put them into something that is going to heaven. Cattle, lands, stocks, bonds and houses will not make it to heaven. Only men, women, boys and girls of all color are going to heaven. By exchanging our earthly possessions and money into the saving of souls, we will take our acquired wealth with us to an eternal home.

The Old Testament believers were required to give a specific amount of money in order to meet the needs of the ministry, the poor, etc. While the New Testament does not specifically mention the tithe as a directive,

II Corinthians 8:3 does direct us to give as we are able and even above and beyond.

Jesus' view on giving was even more radical than tithing! He did not want us to be bound by material things and even said that we should sell our possessions and give all to the poor.

Luke told us to accumulate our treasures in heaven where they would be safe from moths and thieves. When you look closely, the tithe of 10% seems like a minimum giving guideline in the New Testament. The new did not replace the old, but it increased and expanded the giving possibilities.

Abraham tithed before the Law of Moses. The first Biblical record of tithing is found in Genesis 14. Abram's nephew, Lot, was taken captive in a battle between some kings and their armies. When Abram set out to rescue him, not only was he successful, but he also brought back a large amount of spoils. Genesis 14:11-20 records this event.

Giving God back a tenth of what was already His was a way of acknowledging God's ownership of the entire earth's wealth. Haggai 2:8 declares, "The silver is mine, and the gold is mine, saith the LORD of hosts." (KJV). Long before the time of Moses, the dedication of the tenth to God was recognized as a duty. It was consecrated and set apart for special purposes.

Genesis 14:20, 22

And blessed be God Most High, who delivered your enemies into your hand." Then Abram gave him a tenth of everything. But Abram said to the king of Sodom, "I have raised my hand to the LORD, God Most High, Creator of heaven and earth, and have taken an oath. NIV

Malachi 3:10

Bring the whole tithe into the storehouse, that there may be food in my house. Test me in this," says the LORD Almighty, "and see if I will not throw open the floodgates of heaven and pour out so much blessing that you will not have room enough for it. NIV

Matthew 23:23

Woe to you, teachers of the law and Pharisees, you hypocrites! You give a tenth of your spices-mint, dill and cummin. But you have neglected the more important matters of the law-justice, mercy and faithfulness. You should have practiced the latter, without neglecting the former. NIV

Luke 11:42

Woe to you Pharisees, because you give God a tenth of your mint, rue and all other kinds of garden herbs, but you neglect justice and the love of God. You should have practiced the latter without leaving the former undone. NIV

Hebrews 7:1-10

This Melchizedek was king of Salem and priest of God Most High. He met Abraham returning from the defeat of the kings and blessed him, and Abraham gave him a tenth of everything. First, his name means "king of righteousness"; then also, "king of Salem" means "king of peace." Without father or mother, without genealogy, without beginning of days or end of life, like the Son of God he remains a priest forever. Just think how great he was: Even the patriarch Abraham gave him a tenth of the plunder! Now the law requires the descendants of Levi who become priests to collect a tenth from the people-that is, their brothers-even though their brothers are descended from Abraham. This man, however, did not trace his descent from Levi, yet he collected a tenth from Abraham and blessed him who had the promises. And without doubt the lesser person is blessed by the greater. In the one case, the tenth is collected by men who die; but in the other case, by him who is declared to be living. One might even say that Levi, who collects the tenth, paid the tenth through Abraham, because when Melchizedek met Abraham, Levi was still in the body of his ancestor. NIV

Trust

Jeremiah 17:7, 8

But blessed is the man who trusts in the LORD, whose confidence is in him. He will be like a tree planted by the water that sends out its roots by the stream. It does not fear when heat comes; its leaves are always green. It has no worries in a year of drought and never fails to bear fruit." NIV

Mark 6:9

Wear sandals but not an extra tunic. NIV

Mark 8:34

Then he called the crowd to him along with his disciples and said: "If anyone would come after me, he must deny himself and take up his cross and follow me. NIV

Philippians 4:19

And my God will meet all your needs according to his glorious riches in Christ Jesus. NIV

Truthfulness

Psalms 1:1-2

Blessed is the man who does not walk in the counsel of the wicked or stand in the way of sinners or sit in the seat of mockers. But his delight is in the law of the LORD, and on his law he meditates day and night. NIV

Psalms 37:37

Consider the blameless, observe the upright; there is a future for the man of peace. NIV

Psalms 112:6

Surely he will never be shaken; a righteous man will be remembered forever. NIV

Proverbs 10:16

The wages of the righteous bring them life, but the income of the wicked brings them punishment. NIV

Proverbs 11:4

Wealth is worthless in the day of wrath, but righteousness delivers from death. NIV

Proverbs 12:12

The wicked desire the plunder of evil men, but the root of the righteous flourishes. NIV

Proverbs 13:22

A good man leaves an inheritance for his children's children, but a sinner's wealth is stored up for the righteous. NIV

Proverbs 16:8, 11

Better a little with righteousness than much gain with injustice. Honest scales and balances are from the LORD; all the weights in the bag are of his making. NIV

Proverbs 19:1

Better a poor man whose walk is blameless than a fool whose lips are perverse. NIV

Proverbs 21:3

To do what is right and just is more acceptable to the LORD than sacrifice. NIV

Proverbs 22:1

A good name is more desirable than great riches; to be esteemed is better than silver or gold. NIV

Proverbs 28:6, 13

Better a poor man whose walk is blameless than a rich man whose ways are perverse. He who conceals his sins does not prosper, but whoever confesses and renounces them finds mercy. NIV

Matthew 7:20

Thus, by their fruit you will recognize them. NIV

Matthew 17:24

After Jesus and his disciples arrived in Capernaum, the collectors of the two-drachma tax came to Peter and asked, "Doesn't your teacher pay the temple tax?" NIV

Luke 3:12-13

Tax collectors also came to be baptized. "Teacher," they asked, "what should we do?" "Don't collect any more than you are required to," he told them. NIV

Luke 3:14

Then some soldiers asked him, "And what should we do?" He replied, "Don't extort money and don't accuse people falsely-be content with your pay." NIV

Luke 8:15

But the seed on good soil stands for those with a noble and good heart, who hear the word, retain it, and by persevering produce a crop. NIV

Luke 12:58

As you are going with your adversary to the magistrate, try hard to be reconciled to him on the way, or he may drag you off to the judge, and the judge turn you over to the officer, and the officer throw you into prison. NIV

Luke 20:22-25

Keeping a close watch on him, they sent spies, who pretended to be honest. They hoped to catch Jesus in something he said so that they might hand him over to the power and authority of the governor. So the spies questioned him: "Teacher, we know that you speak and teach what is right, and that you do not show partiality but teach the way of God in accordance with the truth. Is it right for us to pay taxes to Caesar or not?" He saw through their duplicity and said to them, "Show me a denarius. Whose portrait and inscription are on it?" "Caesar's," they replied. He said to them, "Then give to Caesar what is Caesar's, and to God what is God's." NIV

Romans 13:7

Give everyone what you owe him: If you owe taxes, pay taxes; if revenue, then revenue; if respect, then respect; if honor, then honor. NIV

Romans 13:9

The commandments, "Do not commit adultery," "Do not murder," "Do not steal," "Do not covet," and whatever other commandment there may be, are summed up in this one rule: "Love your neighbor as yourself." NIV

Galatians 6:9

Let us not become weary in doing good, for at the proper time we will reap a harvest if we do not give up. NIV

Waste

John 6:11-13

> *Jesus then took the loaves, gave thanks, and distributed to those who were seated as much as they wanted. He did the same with the fish. When they had all had enough to eat, he said to his disciples, "Gather the pieces that are left over. Let nothing be wasted." So they gathered them and filled twelve baskets with the pieces of the five barley loaves left over by those who had eaten.*

In the story of the feeding of the five thousand by Christ, He recognized the need of the crowd of people. Knowing that the people were hungry and should be fed He took stock of the available resources. All they could find was a lad with five loaves and two fishes. So Christ used that. Through the miracle of multiplication the entire multitude was fed. Instead of resting in the praise of the contented participants, Jesus was very concerned that there be nothing wasted.

Have you ever wasted the blessing of God? What has God provided miraculously for you that you squandered? What income and finances has He given to you that you let slip away with frivolous spending?

Many people, deep in debt and lacking in self discipline in their spending and contentment level, complain that their employers don't pay them enough, their taxes are much too high, their business costs have skyrocketed, or render some other excuse why they cannot plan for their financial future. Of course, some of these excuses may have a certain amount of legitimacy to them, but they don't excuse a person from the responsibility of "no waste."

The problem is not a lack of money; it is a problem of lack of money management.

In Luke 16, the story is told of a dishonest steward who wasted his lord's goods for which he was liable, and was judged by his master.

In times past, I thought this steward was expelled from his job because of fraud. But the verses do not say this. If it were fraud, the master never would have let him stay around long enough to make alternate arrangements with the master's debtors. The verses simply infer that he was a bad money manager. If the steward had not been so fiscally challenged, the master could have had a better return on his investments, and not wasted the investment return he never received.

Today, we also are responsible to our Master for His creation and blessing. The scope of the parable suggests to us that it is important to manage our possessions and life on earth in such a way that will benefit us in eternal life. It's not that eternal life is our sole reason for managing our possessions judiciously. We should do this from our obedience, appreciation and our love for God.

We are wrong to make bad decisions when we waste the finances God has allowed to flow through our lives. All of us are stewards of what has been entrusted to us. We have a fiduciary responsibility to employ our wealth in acts of charity and good works, seeking an eternal return much the same way the dishonest steward employed his abilities to achieve the greatest temporal profit.

A lot of wasteful spending is incurred on perfectly good purchases, but more often than not, many purchases are for things we neither need nor use. How many attics, basements and garages are full of great buys that were never used? If they were used, maybe they were rarely used. I could tell you about some exercise equipment I purchased that falls into this category. When all is said and done, the amount spent on these items, although seemingly legit, was very wasteful.

Genesis 41:36

This food should be held in reserve for the country, to be used during the seven years of famine that will come upon Egypt, so that the country may not be ruined by the famine." NIV

Wealth

Proverbs 3:9

Honor the LORD with your wealth.

Many readers of this book would not think their lifestyle is one of wealth and excess. To you the words extravagant and excessive would not seem descriptive of your standard of living. But the reality is that most of you really do live a life of abundance; you travel to where you wish, you buy what you desire and there are very few constraints in your lifetime of opportunities.

Dr. Neil Chadwick explains to us how really wealthy some of us are in the country of my origin (USA) in this excerpt from one of his messages.

"Recently it has come to my attention just how imbalanced a world we live in. The fact of the matter is, if you have food in the refrigerator, clothes on your back, a roof overhead and a place to sleep, you are richer than 75% of this world. If you have money in the bank, in your wallet, and spare change in a dish someplace - you are among the top 8% of the world's wealthy. If we could shrink the earth's population to a village of precisely 100 people, with all the existing human ratios remaining the same, 6 people would possess 59% of the entire world's wealth and all 6 would be from the United States; 80 would live in substandard housing; 70 would be unable to read; 50 would suffer from malnutrition; and only 1 would have a college education."

So what do you think about this verse in Proverbs 3:9; "Honor the LORD with your wealth"? Do you think that it applies to someone else? Were you tempted to skip this principle thinking that it was not applicable to you? Don't be so sure that when compared with historical data and the rest of today's world, that you shouldn't take notice. Regardless of whether or not you have great wealth, by the standards of most of the world's citizens, you are a wealthy person.

Genesis 31:1

Now Jacob heard the words of Laban's sons, saying, "Jacob has taken away all that was our father's, and from what was our father's he has acquired all this wealth." NKJV

Genesis 34:29

And all their wealth. All their little ones and their wives they took captive; and they plundered even all that was in the houses. NKJV

Deuteronomy 8:17

Then you say in your heart, 'My power and the might of my hand have gained me this wealth.' NKJV

Deuteronomy 8:18

And you shall remember the LORD your God, for it is He who gives you power to get wealth, that He may establish

All the Financial Scriptures in the Bible with Commentary

His covenant which He swore to your fathers, as it is this day. NKJV

Ruth 2:1

Ruth Meets Boaz, there was a relative of Naomi's husband, a man of great wealth, of the family of Elimelech. His name was Boaz. NKJV

1 Kings 10:14

Solomon's Great Wealth, the weight of gold that came to Solomon yearly was six hundred and sixty-six talents of gold, NKJV

2 Kings 15:20

And Menahem exacted the money from Israel, from all the very wealthy, from each man fifty shekels of silver, to give to the king of Assyria. So the king of Assyria turned back, and did not stay there in the land. NKJV

2 Chronicles 1:11

Then God said to Solomon: "Because this was in your heart, and you have not asked riches or wealth or honor or the life of your enemies, nor have you asked long life -- but have asked wisdom and knowledge for yourself, that you may judge My people over whom I have made you king – NKJV

2 Chronicles 1:12

Wisdom and knowledge are granted to you; and I will give you riches and wealth and honor, such as none of the kings have had who were before you, nor shall any after you have the like." NKJV

2 Chronicles 9:13

The weight of gold that came to Solomon yearly was six hundred and sixty-six talents of gold, NKJV

2 Chronicles 32:27

Hezekiah had very great riches and honor. And he made himself treasuries for silver, for gold, for precious stones, for spices, for shields, and for all kinds of desirable items; NKJV

Job 6:22

Did I ever say, 'Bring something to me'? Or, 'Offer a bribe for me from your wealth'? NKJV

Job 15:29

He will not be rich, nor will his wealth continue, nor will his possessions overspread the earth. NKJV

Job 20:10

His children will seek the favor of the poor, and his hands will restore his wealth. NKJV

Job 21:13

They spend their days in wealth, and in a moment go down to the grave. NKJV

Job 30:1

But now they mock at me, men younger than I, whose fathers I disdained to put with the dogs of my flock. NKJV

Job 31:25

If I have rejoiced because my wealth was great, and because my hand had gained much; NKJV

Psalms 49:6

Those who trust in their wealth, and boast in the multitude of their riches, NKJV

Psalms 49:10

For he sees wise men die; likewise the fool and the senseless person perish, and leave their wealth to others. NKJV

Psalms 112:3

Wealth and riches will be in his house, and his righteousness endures forever. NKJV

Proverbs 5:10

Lest aliens be filled with your wealth, and your labors go to the house of a foreigner; NKJV

Proverbs 8:21

That I may cause those who love me to inherit wealth, that I may fill their treasuries. NKJV

Proverbs 10:15

The rich man's wealth is his strong city; the destruction of the poor is their poverty. NKJV

Proverbs 13:11

Wealth gained by dishonesty will be diminished, but he who gathers by labor will increase. NKJV

Proverbs 13:22

A good man leaves an inheritance to his children's children, but the wealth of the sinner is stored up for the righteous. NKJV

Proverbs 18:11

The rich man's wealth is his strong city, and like a high wall in his own esteem. NKJV

Proverbs 19:4

Wealth makes many friends, but the poor is separated from his friend. NKJV

Proverbs 29:3

Whoever loves wisdom makes his father rejoice, but a companion of harlots wastes his wealth. NKJV

Ecclesiastes 5:19

As for every man to whom God has given riches and wealth, and given him power to eat of it, to receive his heritage and rejoice in his labor -- this is the gift of Go. NKJV

Ecclesiastes 6:1

Wealth Is Not the Goal of Life, there is an evil which I have seen under the sun, and it is common among men: NKJV

Ecclesiastes 6:2

A man to whom God has given riches and wealth and honor, so that he lacks nothing for himself of all he desires; yet God does not give him power to eat of it, but a foreigner consumes it. This is vanity, and it is an evil affliction. NKJV

Song of Solomon 8:7

Many waters cannot quench love, nor can the floods drown it. If a man would give for love, all the wealth of his house, it would be utterly despised. NKJV

Isaiah 60:5

Then you shall see and become radiant, and your heart shall swell with joy; because the abundance of the sea shall be turned to you, the wealth of the Gentiles shall come to you. NKJV

Isaiah 60:11

Therefore your gates shall be open continually; they shall not be shut day or night, that men may bring to you the wealth of the Gentiles, and their kings in procession. NKJV

Jeremiah 15:13

Your wealth and your treasures, I will give as plunder without price, because of all your sins, throughout your territories. NKJV

Jeremiah 17:3

O My mountain in the field, I will give as plunder your wealth, all your treasures, and your high places of sin within all your borders. NKJV

Jeremiah 20:5

Moreover I will deliver all the wealth of this city, all its produce, and all its precious things; all the treasures of the kings of Judah I will give into the hand of their enemies, who will plunder them, seize them, and carry them to Babylon. NKJV

Ezekiel 29:19

Therefore thus says the Lord GOD: 'Surely I will give the land of Egypt to Nebuchadnezzar king of Babylon; he shall take away her wealth, carry off her spoil, and remove her pillage; and that will be the wages for his army. NKJV

Ezekiel 30:4

The sword shall come upon Egypt, and great anguish shall be in Ethiopia, when the slain fall in Egypt, and they take away her wealth, and her foundations are broken down. NKJV

Hosea 12:8

And Ephraim said, 'Surely I have become rich, I have found wealth for myself;In all my labors, they shall find in me no iniquity that is sin.' NKJV

Nahum 2:9

Take spoil of silver! Take spoil of gold! There is no end of treasure, or wealth of every desirable prize. NKJV

Zechariah 14:14

Judah also will fight at Jerusalem. And the wealth of all the surrounding nations Shall be gathered together: Gold, silver, and apparel in great abundance. NKJV

Luke 6:38

Give, and it will be given to you. A good measure, pressed down, shaken together and running over, will be poured into your lap. For with the measure you use, it will be measured to you." NIV

John 10:10

The thief comes only to steal and kill and destroy; I have come that they may have life, and have it to the full. NIV

2 Corinthians 8:9

For you know the grace of our Lord Jesus Christ, that though he was rich, yet for your sakes he became poor, so that you through his poverty might become rich. NIV

All the Financial Scriptures in the Bible with Commentary

Philippians 4:19

And my God will meet all your needs according to his glorious riches in Christ Jesus. NIV

Revelation 3:17

Because you say, 'I am rich, have become wealthy, and have need of nothing'-- and do not know that you are wretched, miserable, poor, blind, and naked-- NKJV

Revelation 18:19

They threw dust on their heads and cried out, weeping and wailing, and saying, 'Alas, alas, that great city, in which all who had ships on the sea became rich by her wealth! For in one hour she is made desolate.' NKJV

Wives

Proverbs 31:10-31

Who can find a virtuous wife? For her worth is far above rubies. The heart of her husband safely trusts her; so he will have no lack of gain. She does him good and not evil All the days of her life. She seeks wool and flax, and willingly works with her hands. She is like the merchant ships, she brings her food from afar. She also rises while it is yet night, and provides food for her household, and a portion for her maidservants. She considers a field and buys it; from her profits she plants a vineyard. She girds herself with strength, and strengthens her arms. She perceives that her merchandise is good, and her lamp does not go out by night. She stretches out her hands to the distaff, and her hand holds the spindle. She extends her hand to the poor, yes, she reaches out her hands to the needy. she is not afraid of snow for her household, for all her household is clothed with scarlet. She makes tapestry for herself; her clothing is fine linen and purple. Her husband is known in the gates, when he sits among the elders of the land. She makes linen garments and sells them, and supplies sashes for the merchants. Strength and honor are her clothing; she shall rejoice in time to come. She opens her mouth with wisdom, and on her tongue is the law of kindness. She watches over the ways of her household, and does not eat the bread of idleness. Her children rise up and call her blessed; her husband also, and he praises her: "Many daughters have done well, but you excel them all."

Charm is deceitful and beauty is passing, but a woman who fears the LORD, she shall be praised. Give her of the fruit of her hands, and let her own works praise her in the gates. NKJV

Work

God's supernatural provision does not replace hard work and persistent labor. Working and doing our part is never an easy task. It is rewarding, but challenging. Only God has the power to speak the word and cause something to happen instantly, but with man, work is necessary to accomplish an end result.

In the book of Genesis, Adam was the sole steward appointed over all natural resources, as well as plant and animal life – a substantial entrustment from God. So when Adam disobeyed and lost that leadership, it affected a lot more than his descendants; it affected the sea, the air, the earth and life as well.

When the steward (Adam) went astray, that which had been entrusted to him was severely injured. According to Romans 8:22, the whole earth groans in travail. When Adam and Eve sinned, God judged them. Humans were required to leave the plush Garden of Eden. God commanded in Genesis 3:19, "In the sweat of thy face shalt thou eat bread, till thou return unto the ground" (KJV).

Robert Ingersoll once said, "Every man is dishonest who lives upon the labor of others, no matter if he occupies a throne."

The famous poet Robert Frost once gave an insightful quotation regarding work and people. He said, "The world is filled with willing people. Some willing to work, and the rest willing to let them."

In the United States, unlike Third World countries, we do not have a lower class. Though many think otherwise, all healthy people who want to work can do so, provide for themselves, have plenty to eat and shelter for sleep. There are, of course, economic cycles of employment, job availability, discomfort and times when growth opportunity is limited. When compared to the poor of this world, however, those who lack the most in this country are far better off than almost anyone anywhere else in the world.

In the Western world, a great deal of emphasis is placed upon having fun, spending time in leisurely activity and taking care of the whims of "me." Many are content to put as little into their work as they think they can get away with. Far too many employees are receiving a full paycheck for less than a full day's work. Scriptures note in 2 Thessalonians 3:10, "if any would not work, neither should he eat" (KJV).

Deuteronomy 24:14-15

You shall not oppress a hired servant who is poor and needy, whether one of your brethren or one of the aliens who is in your land within your gates. Each day you shall give him his wages, and not let the sun go down on it, for he is poor and has set his heart on it; lest he cry out against you to the LORD, and it be sin to you. NKJV

Proverbs 6:6-10

Go to the ant, you sluggard! Consider her ways and be wise, which, having no captain, overseer or ruler, provides her supplies in the summer, and gathers her food in the harvest. How long will you slumber, O sluggard? When will you rise from your sleep? A little sleep, a little slumber, a little folding of the hands to sleep — NKJV

Proverbs 10:4-5

He who has a slack hand becomes poor, but the hand of the diligent makes rich. He who gathers in summer is a wise son; he who sleeps in harvest is a son who causes shame. NKJV

Proverbs 12:11,24

He who tills his land will be satisfied with bread, but he who follows frivolity is devoid of understanding. The hand of the diligent will rule, but the lazy man will be put to forced labor. NKJV

Proverbs 14:23

In all labor there is profit, but idle chatter leads only to poverty. NKJV

Proverbs 16:26

The person who labors, labors for himself, for his hungry mouth drives him on. NKJV

Proverbs 28:19

He who tills his land will have plenty of bread, but he who follows frivolity will have poverty enough! NKJV

Ephesians 4:28

Let him who stole steal no longer, but rather let him labor, working with his hands what is good, that he may have something to give him who has need. NKJV

Worry

Psalm 37:25

I was young and now I am old, yet I have never seen the righteous forsaken or their children begging bread.

Worry is the opposite of faith. A Christian cannot be filled with faith and worry at the same time. The psalmist David had plenty of times when he could have been filled with worry…even to the point of wondering if his enemies would kill him. Even Jesus taught us to ask for our daily bread. He is more than willing to provide for us but apparently is very adamant that we ask for his help first. God never abandons His children. He always provides for them. In His time, God will always right the wrongs, avenge injustice and keep His promises.

God will provide for you through many natural resources available to Him. In addition to the ongoing natural resources that He has placed on the earth, when desirable He will provide for us through supernatural means. He fed the prophet Elijah with food sent by ravens. He fed the five thousand men plus women and children from a few meager morsels of food.

When we were children, we never worried about our parents providing for us. My parents provided me with a warm bed, daily food and a roof over my head. Nothing was left to chance. In this manner our Heavenly Father provides for our needs daily. Day after day, month after month He proves His love for us even knowing our needs before we ask Him.

All the Financial Scriptures in the Bible with Commentary

Psalms 50:14-15

Offer to God thanksgiving, and pay your vows to the Most High. Call upon Me in the day of trouble; I will deliver you, and you shall glorify Me." NKJV

Psalm 115:12

The LORD remembers us and will bless us:

Proverbs 3:5

Trust in the LORD with all your heart and lean not on your own understanding;

Proverbs 12:25

Anxiety in the heart of man causes depression, but a good word makes it glad. NKJV

Matthew 6:27-34

Which of you by worrying can add one cubit to his stature? So why do you worry about clothing? Consider the lilies of the field, how they grow: they neither toil nor spin; and yet I say to you that even Solomon in all his glory was not arrayed like one of these. Now if God so clothes the grass of the field, which today is, and tomorrow is thrown into the oven, will He not much more clothe you, O you of little faith? Therefore do not worry, saying, 'What shall we eat?' or 'What shall we drink?' or 'What shall we wear?' For after all these things the Gentiles seek. For your heavenly Father knows that you need all these things. But seek first the kingdom of God and His righteousness, and all these things shall be added to you. Therefore do not worry about tomorrow, for tomorrow will worry about its own things. Sufficient for the day is its own trouble. NKJV

Philippians 4:6

Be anxious for nothing, but in everything by prayer and supplication, with thanksgiving, let your requests be made known to God; NKJV

1 Peter 5:7

Cast all your anxiety on him because he cares for you.

1 John 4:18

There is no fear in love; but perfect love casts out fear, because fear involves torment. But he who fears has not been made perfect in love. NKJV

Scriptural References on Offerings

All the Financial Scriptures in the Bible with Commentary

Offering

2 Corinthians 9:7

Every man according as he purposeth in his heart, so let him give; not grudgingly, or of necessity: for God loveth a cheerful giver. (KJV)

What kind of a giver are you? Are you a person who gives grudgingly or are you the kind of person that God loves; a cheerful giver. A cheerful giver receives great happiness; so much that the giver's own challenges and personal pain is soon forgotten. This is the story of one such giver.

This story is about a beautiful, expensively dressed lady who complained to her psychiatrist that she felt that her whole life was empty; it had no meaning. So the counselor called over the old lady who cleaned the office floors, and then said to the rich lady, "I'm going to ask Mary here to tell you how she found happiness. All I want you to do is listen."

So the old lady put down her broom and sat on a chair and told her story: "Well, my husband died of malaria and three months later my only son was killed by a car. I had nobody... I had nothing left. I couldn't sleep; I couldn't eat; I never smiled at anyone, I even thought of taking my own life. Then one evening a little kitten followed me home from work. Somehow I felt sorry for that kitten. It was cold outside, so I decided to let the kitten in. I got it some milk, and it licked the plate clean. Then it purred and rubbed against my leg, and for the first time in months, I smiled.

Then I stopped to think; if helping a little kitten could make me smile, maybe doing something for people could make me happy. So the next day I baked some biscuits and took them to a neighbor who was sick in bed. Every day I tried to do something nice for someone. It made me so happy to see them happy. Today, I don't know of anybody who sleeps and eats better than I do. I've found happiness, by giving it to others."

When she heard that, the rich lady cried. She had everything that money could buy, but she had lost the things which money cannot buy.
Source Unknown

Genesis 4:3

And in process of time it came to pass, that Cain brought of the fruit of the ground an offering unto Jehovah. ASV

Genesis 4:4

And Abel, he also brought of the firstlings of his flock and of the fat thereof. And Jehovah had respect unto Abel and to his offering: ASV

Genesis 4:5

but unto Cain and to his offering he had not respect. And Cain was very wroth, and his countenance fell. ASV

Genesis 22:2

And he said, Take now thy son, thine only son, whom thou lovest, even Isaac, and get thee into the land of Moriah. And offer him there for a burnt-offering upon one of the mountains which I will tell thee of. ASV

Genesis 22:3

And Abraham rose early in the morning, and saddled his ass, and took two of his young men with him, and Isaac his son. And he clave the wood for the burnt-offering, and rose up, and went unto the place of which God had told him. ASV

Genesis 22:6

And Abraham took the wood of the burnt-offering, and laid it upon Isaac his son. And he took in his hand the fire and the knife. And they went both of them together. ASV

Genesis 22:7

And Isaac spake unto Abraham his father, and said, My father. And he said, Here am I, my son. And he said, Behold, the fire and the wood. But where is the lamb for a burnt-offering? ASV

Genesis 22:8

And Abraham said, God will provide himself the lamb for a burnt-offering, my son. So they went both of them together. ASV

Genesis 22:13

And Abraham lifted up his eyes, and looked, and behold, behind (him) a ram caught in the thicket by his horns. And Abraham went and took the ram, and offered him up for a burnt-offering in the stead of his son. ASV

Genesis 35:14

And Jacob set up a pillar in the place where he spake with him, a pillar of stone: and he poured out a drink-offering thereon, and poured oil thereon. ASV

Exodus 18:12

And Jethro, Moses' father-in-law, took a burnt-offering and sacrifices for God: and Aaron came, and all the elders of Israel, to eat bread with Moses' father-in-law before God. ASV

Exodus 25:2

Speak unto the children of Israel, that they take for me an offering: of every man whose heart maketh him willing ye shall take my offering. ASV

Exodus 25:3

And this is the offering which ye shall take of them: gold, and silver, and brass, ASV

Exodus 29:14

But the flesh of the bullock, and its skin, and its dung, shalt thou burn with fire without the camp: it is a sin-offering. ASV

Exodus 29:18

And thou shalt burn the whole ram upon the altar: it is a burnt-offering unto Jehovah; it is a sweet savor, an offering made by fire unto Jehovah. ASV

Exodus 29:24

And thou shalt put the whole upon the hands of Aaron, and upon the hands of his sons, and shalt wave them for a wave-offering before Jehovah. ASV

Exodus 29:25

And thou shalt take them from their hands, and burn them on the altar upon the burnt-offering, for a sweet savor before Jehovah: it is an offering made by fire unto Jehovah. ASV

Exodus 29:26

And thou shalt take the breast of Aaron's ram of consecration, and wave it for a wave-offering before Jehovah: and it shall be thy portion. ASV

Exodus 29:27

And thou shalt sanctify the breast of the wave-offering, and the thigh of the heave-offering, which is waved, and which is heaved up, of the ram of consecration, even of that which is for Aaron, and of that which is for his sons: ASV

Exodus 29:28

And it shall be for Aaron and his sons as (their) portion for ever from the children of Israel; for it is a heave-offering: and it shall be a heave-offering from the children of Israel of the sacrifices of their peace-offerings, even their heave-offering unto Jehovah. ASV

Exodus 29:36

And every day shalt thou offer the bullock of sin-offering for atonement: and thou shalt cleanse the altar, when thou makest atonement for it; and thou shalt anoint it, to sanctify it. ASV

Exodus 29:40

and with the one lamb a tenth part (of an ephah) of fine flour mingled with the fourth part of a hin of beaten oil, and the fourth part of a hin of wine for a drink-offering. ASV

Exodus 29:41

And the other lamb thou shalt offer at even, and shalt do thereto according to the meal-offering of the morning, and according to the drink-offering thereof, for a sweet savor, an offering made by fire unto Jehovah. ASV

Exodus 29:42

It shall be a continual burnt-offering throughout your generations at the door of the tent of meeting before Jehovah, where I will meet with you, to speak there unto thee. ASV

Exodus 30:9

Ye shall offer no strange incense thereon, nor burnt-offering, nor meal-offering; and ye shall pour no drink-offering thereon. ASV

Exodus 30:10

And Aaron shall make atonement upon the horns of it once in the year; with the blood of the sin-offering of atonement once in the year shall he make atonement for it throughout your generations: it is most holy unto Jehovah. ASV

Exodus 30:13

This they shall give, every one that passeth over unto them that are numbered, half a shekel after the shekel of the sanc-

tuary; (the shekel is twenty gerahs;) half a shekel for an offering to Jehovah. ASV

Exodus 30:14

Every one that passeth over unto them that are numbered, from twenty years old and upward, shall give the offering of Jehovah. ASV

Exodus 30:15

The rich shall not give more, and the poor shall not give less, than the half shekel, when they give the offering of Jehovah, to make atonement for your souls. ASV

Exodus 30:20

when they go into the tent of meeting, they shall wash with water, that they die not; or when they come near to the altar to minister, to burn an offering made by fire unto Jehovah. ASV

Exodus 30:28

and the altar of burnt-offering with all the vessels thereof, and the laver and the base thereof. ASV

Exodus 31:9

And the altar of burnt-offering with all its vessels, and the laver and its base, ASV

Exodus 32:6

And they rose up early on the morrow, and offered burnt-offerings, and brought peace-offerings; and the people sat down to eat and to drink, and rose up to play. ASV

Exodus 35:5

Take ye from among you an offering unto Jehovah; whosoever is of a willing heart, let him bring it, Jehovah's offering: gold, and silver, and brass, ASV

Exodus 35:16

the altar of burnt-offering, with its grating of brass, it staves, and all its vessels, the laver and its base; ASV

Exodus 35:21

And they came, every one whose heart stirred him up, and every one whom his spirit made willing, (and) brought Jehovah's offering, for the work of the tent of meeting, and for all the service thereof, and for the holy garments. ASV

Exodus 35:22

And they came, both men and women, as many as were willing-hearted, (and) brought brooches, and ear-rings, and signet-rings, and armlets, all jewels of gold; even every man that offered an offering of gold unto Jehovah. ASV

Exodus 35:24

Every one that did offer an offering of silver and brass brought Jehovah's offering; and every man, with whom was found acacia wood for any work of the service, brought it. ASV

Exodus 35:29

The children of Israel brought a freewill-offering unto Jehovah; every man and woman, whose heart made them willing to bring for all the work, which Jehovah had commanded to be made by Moses. ASV

Exodus 36:3

And they received of Moses all the offering which the children of Israel had brought for the work of the service of the sanctuary, wherewith to make it. And they brought yet unto him freewill-offerings every morning. ASV

Exodus 36:6

And Moses gave commandment, and they caused it to be proclaimed throughout the camp, saying, Let neither man nor woman make any more work for the offering of the sanctuary. So the people were restrained from bringing. ASV

Exodus 38:1

And he made the altar of burnt-offering of acacia wood: five cubits was the length thereof, and five cubits the breadth thereof, foursquare; and three cubits the height thereof. ASV

Exodus 38:24

All the gold that was used for the work in all the work of the sanctuary, even the gold of the offering, was twenty and nine talents, and seven hundred and thirty shekels, after the shekel of the sanctuary. ASV

Exodus 38:29

And the brass of the offering was seventy talents, and two thousand and four hundred shekels. ASV

Exodus 40:6

And thou shalt set the altar of burnt-offering before the door of the tabernacle of the tent of meeting. ASV

Exodus 40:10

And thou shalt anoint the altar of burnt-offering, and all its vessels, and sanctify the altar: and the altar shall be most holy. ASV

Exodus 40:29

And he set the altar of burnt-offering at the door of the tabernacle of the tent of meeting, and offered upon it the burnt-offering and the meal-offering; as Jehovah commanded Moses. ASV

Leviticus 1:2

Speak unto the children of Israel, and say unto them, When any man of you offereth an oblation unto Jehovah, ye shall offer your oblation of the cattle, (even) of the herd and of the flock. ASV

Leviticus 1:3

If his oblation be a burnt-offering of the herd, he shall offer it a male without blemish: he shall offer it at the door of the tent of meeting, that he may be accepted before Jehovah. ASV

Leviticus 1:4

And he shall lay his hand upon the head of the burnt-offering; and it shall be accepted for him to make atonement for him. ASV

Leviticus 1:6

And he shall flay the burnt-offering, and cut it into its pieces. ASV

Leviticus 1:9

but its inwards and its legs shall he wash with water: and the priest shall burn the whole on the altar, for a burnt-offering, an offering made by fire, of a sweet savor unto Jehovah. ASV

Leviticus 1:10

And if his oblation be of the flock, of the sheep, or of the goats, for a burnt-offering; he shall offer it a male without blemish. ASV

Leviticus 1:13

but the inwards and the legs shall he wash with water; and the priest shall offer the whole, and burn it upon the altar: it is a burnt-offering, an offering made by fire, of a sweet savor unto Jehovah. ASV

Leviticus 1:14

And if his oblation to Jehovah be a burnt-offering of birds, then he shall offer his oblation of turtle-doves, or of young pigeons. ASV

Leviticus 1:17

And he shall rend it by the wings thereof, (but) shall not divide it asunder; and the priest shall burn it upon the altar, upon the wood that is upon the fire: it is a burnt-offering, an offering made by fire, of a sweet savor unto Jehovah. ASV

Leviticus 2:1

And when any one offereth an oblation of a meal-offering unto Jehovah, his oblation shall be of fine flour; and he shall pour oil upon it, and put frankincense thereon: ASV

Leviticus 2:2

And he shall bring it to Aaron's sons the priests; and he shall take thereout his handful of the fine flour thereof, and of the oil thereof, with all the frankincense thereof; and the priest shall burn (it as) the memorial thereof upon the altar, an offering made by fire, of a sweet savor unto Jehovah: ASV

Leviticus 2:3

And that which is left of the meal-offering shall be Aaron's and his sons': it is a thing most holy of the offerings of Jehovah made by fire. ASV

Leviticus 2:4

And when thou offerest an oblation of a meal-offering baken in the oven, it shall be unleavened cakes of fine flour mingled with oil, or unleavened wafers anointed with oil. ASV

Leviticus 2:5

And if thy oblation be a meal-offering of the baking-pan, it shall be of fine flour unleavened, mingled with oil. ASV

Leviticus 2:6

Thou shalt part it in pieces, and pour oil thereon: it is a meal-offering. ASV

Leviticus 2:7

Shall be made of fine flour with oil. ASV

Leviticus 2:8

And thou shalt bring the meal-offering that is made of these things unto Jehovah: and it shall be presented unto the priest, and he shall bring it unto the altar. ASV

Leviticus 2:9

And the priest shall take up from the meal-offering the memorial thereof, and shall burn it upon the altar, an offering made by fire, of a sweet savor unto Jehovah. ASV

Leviticus 2:10

And that which is left of the meal-offering shall be Aaron's and his sons': it is a thing most holy of the offerings of Jehovah made by fire. ASV

Leviticus 2:11

No meal-offering, which ye shall offer unto Jehovah, shallbe made with leaven; for ye shall burn no leaven, nor any honey, as an offering made by fire unto Jehovah. ASV

Leviticus 2:12

As an oblation of firstfruits) ye shall offer them unto Jehovah: but they shall not come up for a sweet savor on the altar. ASV

Leviticus 2:13

And every oblation of thy meal-offering shalt thou season with salt; neither shalt thou suffer the salt of the covenant of thy God to be lacking from thy meal-offering: with all thine oblations thou shalt offer salt. ASV

Leviticus 2:14

And if thou offer a meal-offering of first-fruits unto Jehovah, thou shalt offer for the meal-offering of thy first-fruits grain in the ear parched with fire, bruised grain of the fresh ear. ASV

Leviticus 2:15

And thou shalt put oil upon it, and lay frankincense thereon: it is a meal-offering. ASV

Leviticus 2:16

And the priest shall burn the memorial of it, part of the bruised grain thereof, and part of the oil thereof, with all the frankincense thereof: it is an offering made by fire unto Jehovah. ASV

Leviticus 3:1

And if his oblation be a sacrifice of peace-offerings; if he offer of the herd, whether male or female, he shall offer it without blemish before Jehovah. ASV

Leviticus 3:2

And he shall lay his hand upon the head of his oblation, and kill it at the door of the tent of meeting: and Aaron's sons the priests shall sprinkle the blood upon the altar round about. ASV

Leviticus 3:3

And he shall offer of the sacrifice of peace-offerings an offering made by fire unto Jehovah; the fat that covereth the inwards, and all the fat that is upon the inwards, ASV

Leviticus 3:5

And Aaron's sons shall burn it on the altar upon the burnt-offering, which is upon the wood that is on the fire: it is an offering made by fire, of a sweet savor unto Jehovah. ASV

Leviticus 3:6

And if his oblation for a sacrifice of peace-offerings unto Jehovah be of the flock; male or female, he shall offer it without blemish. ASV

Leviticus 3:7

If he offer a lamb for his oblation, then shall he offer it before Jehovah; ASV

Leviticus 3:8

And he shall lay his hand upon the head of his oblation, and kill it before the tent of meeting: and Aaron's sons shall sprinkle the blood thereof upon the altar round about. ASV

Leviticus 3:9

And he shall offer of the sacrifice of peace-offerings an offering made by fire unto Jehovah; the fat thereof, the fat tail entire, he shall take away hard by the backbone; and the fat that covereth the inwards, and all the fat that is upon the inwards, ASV

Leviticus 3:11

And the priest shall burn it upon the altar: it is the food of the offering made by fire unto Jehovah. ASV

Leviticus 3:12

And if his oblation be a goat, then he shall offer it before Jehovah: ASV

Leviticus 3:14

And he shall offer thereof his oblation, (even) an offering made by fire unto Jehovah; the fat that covereth the inwards, and all the fat that is upon the inwards, ASV

Leviticus 3:16

And the priest shall burn them upon the altar: it is the food of the offering made by fire, for a sweet savor; all the fat is Jehovah's. ASV

Leviticus 4:3

If the anointed priest shall sin so as to bring guilt on the people, then let him offer for his sin, which he hath sinned, a young bullock without blemish unto Jehovah for a sin-offering. ASV

Leviticus 4:7

And the priest shall put of the blood upon the horns of the altar of sweet incense before Jehovah, which is in the tent of meeting; and all the blood of the bullock shall he pour out at the base of the altar of burnt-offering, which is at the door of the tent of meeting. ASV

Leviticus 4:8

And all the fat of the bullock of the sin-offering he shall take off from it; the fat that covereth the inwards, and all the fat that is upon the inwards, ASV

Leviticus 4:10

As it is taken off from the ox of the sacrifice of peace-offerings: and the priest shall burn them upon the altar of burnt-offering. ASV

Leviticus 4:18

And he shall put of the blood upon the horns of the altar which is before Jehovah, that is in the tent of meeting; and all the blood shall he pour out at the base of the altar of burnt-offering, which is at the door of the tent of meeting. ASV

Leviticus 4:20

Thus shall he do with the bullock; as he did with the bullock of the sin-offering, so shall he do with this; and the priest shall make atonement for them, and they shall be forgiven. ASV

Leviticus 4:21

And he shall carry forth the bullock without the camp, and burn it as he burned the first bullock: it is the sin-offering for the assembly. ASV

Leviticus 4:23

If his sin, wherein he hath sinned, be made known to him, he shall bring for his oblation a goat, a male without blemish; ASV

Leviticus 4:24

And he shall lay his hand upon the head of the goat, and kill it in the place where they kill the burnt-offering before Jehovah: it is a sin-offering. ASV

Leviticus 4:25

And the priest shall take of the blood of the sin-offering with his finger, and put it upon the horns of the altar of burnt-offering; and the blood thereof shall he pour out at the base of the altar of burnt-offering. ASV

Leviticus 4:26

And all the fat thereof shall he burn upon the altar, as the fat of the sacrifice of peace-offerings; and the priest shall make atonement for him as concerning his sin, and he shall be forgiven. ASV

Leviticus 4:28

if his sin, which he hath sinned, be made known to him, then he shall bring for his oblation a goat, a female without blemish, for his sin which he hath sinned. ASV

Leviticus 4:29

And he shall lay his hand upon the head of the sin-offering, and kill the sin-offering in the place of burnt-offering. ASV

Leviticus 4:30

And the priest shall take of the blood thereof with his finger, and put it upon the horns of the altar of burnt-offering; and all the blood thereof shall he pour out at the base of the altar. ASV

Leviticus 4:31

he fat thereof shall he take away, as the fat is taken away from off the sacrifice of peace-offerings; and the priest shall burn it upon the altar for a sweet savor unto Jehovah; and the priest shall make atonement for him, and he shall be forgiven. ASV

Leviticus 4:32

And if he bring a lamb as his oblation for a sin-offering, he shall bring it a female without blemish. ASV

Leviticus 4:33

And he shall lay his hand upon the head of the sin-offering, and kill it for a sin-offering in the place where they kill the burnt-offering. ASV

Leviticus 4:34

And the priest shall take of the blood of the sin-offering with his finger, and put it upon the horns of the altar of burnt-offering; and all the blood thereof shall he pour out at the base of the altar: ASV

Leviticus 4:35

And all the fat thereof shall he take away, as the fat of the lamb is taken away from the sacrifice of peace-offerings; and the priest shall burn them on the altar, upon the offerings of Jehovah made by fire; and the priest shall make atonement for him as touching his sin that he hath sinned, and he shall be forgiven. ASV

Leviticus 5:6

And he shall bring his trespass-offering unto Jehovah for his sin which he hath sinned, a female from the flock, a lamb or a goat, for a sin-offering; and the priest shall make atonement for him as concerning his sin. ASV

Leviticus 5:7

And if his means suffice not for a lamb, then he shall bring his trespass-offering for that wherein he hath sinned, two turtle-doves, or two young pigeons, unto Jehovah; one for a sin-offering, and the other for a burnt-offering. ASV

Leviticus 5:8

And he shall bring them unto the priest, who shall offer that which is for the sin-offering first, and wring off its head from its neck, but shall not divide it asunder: ASV

Leviticus 5:9

And he shall sprinkle of the blood of the sin-offering upon the side of the altar; and the rest of the blood shall be drained out at the base of the altar: it is a sin-offering. ASV

Leviticus 5:10

all offer the second for a burnt-offering, according to the ordinance; and the priest shall make atonement for him as concerning his sin which he hath sinned, and he shall be forgiven. ASV

Leviticus 5:11

But if his means suffice not for two turtle-doves, or two young pigeons, then he shall bring his oblation for that wherein he hath sinned, the tenth part of an ephah of fine flour for a sin-offering: he shall put no oil upon it, neither shall he put any frankincense thereon; for it is a sin-offering. ASV

Leviticus 5:12

And he shall bring it to the priest, and the priest shall take his handful of it as the memorial thereof, and burn it on the altar, upon the offerings of Jehovah made by fire: it is a sin-offering. ASV

Leviticus 5:13

And the priest shall make atonement for him as touching his sin that he hath sinned in any of these things, and he shall be forgiven: and (the remnant) shall be the priest's, as the meal-offering. ASV

Leviticus 5:15

If any one commit a trespass, and sin unwittingly, in the holy things of Jehovah; then he shall bring his trespass-offering unto Jehovah, a ram without blemish out of the flock, according to thy estimation in silver by shekels, after the shekel of the sanctuary, for a trespass-offering: ASV

Leviticus 5:16

And he shall make restitution for that which he hath done amiss in the holy thing, and shall add the fifth part thereto, and give it unto the priest; and the priest shall make atonement for him with the ram of the trespass-offering, and he shall be forgiven. ASV

Leviticus 5:18

And he shall bring a ram without blemish out of the flock, according to thy estimation, for a trespass-offering, unto the priest; and the priest shall make atonement for him concern-

ing the thing wherein he erred unwittingly and knew it not, and he shall be forgiven. ASV

Leviticus 5:19

It is a trespass-offering: he is certainly guilty before Jehovah. ASV

Leviticus 6:5

Or any thing about which he hath sworn falsely; he shall even restore it in full, and shall add the fifth part more thereto: unto him to whom it appertaineth shall he give it, in the day of his being found guilty. ASV

Leviticus 6:6

And he shall bring his trespass-offering unto Jehovah, a ram without blemish out of the flock, according to thy estimation, for a trespass-offering, unto the priest: ASV

Leviticus 6:9

Command Aaron and his sons, saying, This is the law of the burnt-offering: the burnt-offering shall be on the hearth upon the altar all night unto the morning; and the fire of the altar shall be kept burning thereon. ASV

Leviticus 6:10

And the priest shall put on his linen garment, and his linen breeches shall he put upon his flesh; and he shall take up the ashes whereto the fire hath consumed the burnt-offering on the altar, and he shall put them beside the altar. ASV

Leviticus 6:12

And the fire upon the altar shall be kept burning thereon, it shall not go out; and the priest shall burn wood on it every morning: and he shall lay the burnt-offering in order upon it, and shall burn thereon the fat of the peace-offerings. ASV

Leviticus 6:14

And this is the law of the meal-offering: the sons of Aaron shall offer it before Jehovah, before the altar. ASV

Leviticus 6:15

And he shall take up therefrom his handful, of the fine flour of the meal-offering, and of the oil thereof, and all the frankincense which is upon the meal-offering, and shall burn it upon the altar for a sweet savor, as the memorial thereof, unto Jehovah. ASV

Leviticus 6:17

It shall not be baken with leaven. I have given it as their portion of my offerings made by fire; it is most holy, as the sin-offering, and as the trespass-offering. ASV

Leviticus 6:20

This is the oblation of Aaron and of his sons, which they shall offer unto Jehovah in the day when he is anointed: the tenth part of an ephah of fine flour for a meal-offering perpetually, half of it in the morning, and half thereof in the evening. ASV

Leviticus 6:21

On a baking-pan it shall be made with oil; when it is soaked, thou shalt bring it in: in baken pieces shalt thou offer the meal-offering for a sweet savor unto Jehovah. ASV

Leviticus 6:23

And every meal-offering of the priest shall be wholly burnt: it shall not be eaten. ASV

Leviticus 6:25

Speak unto Aaron and to his sons, saying, This is the law of the sin-offering: in the place where the burnt-offering is killed shall the sin-offering be killed before Jehovah: it is most holy. ASV

Leviticus 6:30

And no sin-offering, whereof any of the blood is brought into the tent of meeting to make atonement in the holy place, shall be eaten: it shall be burnt with fire. ASV

Leviticus 7:1

And this is the law of the trespass-offering: it is most holy. ASV

Leviticus 7:2

In the place where they kill the burnt-offering shall they kill the trespass-offering; and the blood thereof shall he sprinkle upon the altar round about. ASV

Leviticus 7:5

And the priest shall burn them upon the altar for an offering made by fire unto Jehovah: it is a trespass-offering. ASV

Leviticus 7:7

As is the sin-offering, so is the trespass-offering; there is one law for them: the priest that maketh atonement therewith, he shall have it. ASV

Leviticus 7:8

And the priest that offereth any man's burnt-offering, even the priest shall have to himself the skin of the burnt-offering which he hath offered. ASV

Leviticus 7:9

And every meal-offering that is baken in the oven, and all that is dressed in the frying-pan, and on the baking-pan, shall be the priest's that offereth it. ASV

Leviticus 7:10

And every meal-offering, mingled with oil, or dry, shall all the sons of Aaron have, one as well as another. ASV

Leviticus 7:13

With cakes of leavened bread he shall offer his oblation with the sacrifice of his peace-offerings for thanksgiving. ASV

Leviticus 7:14

And of it he shall offer one out of each oblation for a heave-offering unto Jehovah; it shall be the priest's that sprinkleth the blood of the peace-offerings. ASV

Leviticus 7:15

And the flesh of the sacrifice of his peace-offerings for thanksgiving shall be eaten on the day of his oblation; he shall not leave any of it until the morning. ASV

Leviticus 7:16

But if the sacrifice of his oblation be a vow, or a freewill-offering, it shall be eaten on the day that he offereth his sacrifice; and on the morrow that which remaineth of it shall be eaten: ASV

Leviticus 7:18

And if any of the flesh of the sacrifice of his peace-offerings be eaten on the third day, it shall not be accepted, neither shall it be imputed unto him that offereth it: it shall be an abomination, and the soul that eateth of it shall bear his iniquity. ASV

Leviticus 7:20

But the soul that eateth of the flesh of the sacrifice of peace-offerings, that pertain unto Jehovah, having his uncleanness upon him, that soul shall be cut off from his people. ASV

Leviticus 7:21

And when any one shall touch any unclean thing, the uncleanness of man, or an unclean beast, or any unclean abomination, and eat of the flesh of the sacrifice of peace-offerings, which pertain unto Jehovah, that soul shall be cut off from his people. ASV

Leviticus 7:25

For whosoever eateth the fat of the beast, of which men offer an offering made by fire unto Jehovah, even the soul that eateth it shall be cut off from his people. ASV

Leviticus 7:29

Speak unto the children of Israel, saying, He that offereth the sacrifice of his peace-offerings unto Jehovah shall bring his oblation unto Jehovah out of the sacrifice of his peace-offerings: ASV

Leviticus 7:30

His own hands shall bring the offerings of Jehovah made by fire; the fat with the breast shall he bring, that the breast may be waved for a wave-offering before Jehovah. ASV

Leviticus 7:32

And the right thigh shall ye give unto the priest for a heave-offering out of the sacrifices of your peace-offerings. ASV

Leviticus 7:33

He among the sons of Aaron that offereth the blood of the peace-offerings, and the fat, shall have the right thigh for a portion. ASV

Leviticus 7:34

For the wave-breast and the heave-thigh have I taken of the children of Israel out of the sacrifices of their peace-offerings, and have given them unto Aaron the priest and unto his sons as (their) portion for ever from the children of Israel. ASV

Leviticus 7:37

This is the law of the burnt-offering, of the meal-offering, and of the sin-offering, and of the trespass-offering, and of the consecration, and of the sacrifice of peace-offerings; ASV

Leviticus 8:2

Take Aaron and his sons with him, and the garments, and the anointing oil, and the bullock of the sin-offering, and the two rams, and the basket of unleavened bread; ASV

Leviticus 8:14

And he brought the bullock of the sin-offering: and Aaron and his sons laid their hands upon the head of the bullock of the sin-offering. ASV

Leviticus 8:18

And he presented the ram of the burnt-offering: and Aaron and his sons laid their hands upon the head of the ram. ASV

Leviticus 8:21

And he washed the inwards and the legs with water; and Moses burnt the whole ram upon the altar: it was a burnt-offering for a sweet savor: it was an offering made by fire unto Jehovah; as Jehovah commanded Moses. ASV

Leviticus 8:27

And he put the whole upon the hands of Aaron, and upon the hands of his sons, and waved them for a wave-offering before Jehovah. ASV

Leviticus 8:28

And Moses took them from off their hands, and burnt them on the altar upon the burnt-offering: they were a consecration for a sweet savor: it was an offering made by fire unto Jehovah. ASV

Leviticus 8:29

And Moses took the breast, and waved it for a wave-offering before Jehovah: it was Moses' portion of the ram of consecration; as Jehovah commanded Moses. ASV

Leviticus 9:2

And he said unto Aaron, Take thee a calf of the herd for a sin-offering, and a ram for a burnt-offering, without blemish, and offer them before Jehovah. ASV

Leviticus 9:3

And unto the children of Israel thou shalt speak, saying, Take ye a he-goat for a sin-offering; and a calf and a lamb, both a year old, without blemish, for a burnt-offering; ASV

Leviticus 9:4

And an ox and a ram for peace-offerings, to sacrifice before Jehovah; and a meal-offering mingled with oil: for to-day Jehovah appeareth unto you. ASV

Leviticus 9:7

And Moses said unto Aaron, Draw near unto the altar, and offer thy sin-offering, and thy burnt-offering, and make atonement for thyself, and for the people; and offer the oblation of the people, and make atonement for them; as Jehovah commanded. ASV

All the Financial Scriptures in the Bible with Commentary

Leviticus 9:8

So Aaron drew near unto the altar, and slew the calf of the sin-offering, which was for himself. ASV

Leviticus 9:10

But the fat, and the kidneys, and the caul from the liver of the sin-offering, he burnt upon the altar; as Jehovah commanded Moses. ASV

Leviticus 9:12

And he slew the burnt-offering; and Aaron's sons delivered unto him the blood, and he sprinkled it upon the altar round about. ASV

Leviticus 9:14

And he washed the inwards and the legs, and burnt them upon the burnt-offering on the altar. ASV

Leviticus 9:15

And he presented the people's oblation, and took the goat of the sin-offering which was for the people, and slew it, and offered it for sin, as the first. ASV

Leviticus 9:16

And he presented the burnt-offering, and offered it according to the ordinance. ASV

Leviticus 9:17

And he presented the meal-offering, and filled his hand therefrom, and burnt it upon the altar, besides the burnt-offering of the morning. ASV

Leviticus 9:21

And the breasts and the right thigh Aaron waved for a wave-offering before Jehovah; as Moses commanded. ASV

Leviticus 9:22

And Aaron lifted up his hands toward the people, and blessed them; and he came down from offering the sin-offering, and the burnt-offering, and the peace-offerings. ASV

Leviticus 9:24

And there came forth fire from before Jehovah, and consumed upon the altar the burnt-offering and the fat: and when all the people saw it, they shouted, and fell on their faces. ASV

Leviticus 10:12

And Moses spake unto Aaron, and unto Eleazar and unto Ithamar, his sons that were left, Take the meal-offering that remaineth of the offerings of Jehovah made by fire, and eat it without leaven beside the altar; for it is most holy; ASV

Leviticus 10:14

And the wave-breast and the heave-thigh shall ye eat in a clean place, thou, and thy sons, and thy daughters with thee: for they are given as thy portion, and thy sons' portion, out of the sacrifices of the peace-offerings of the children of Israel. ASV

Leviticus 10:15

The heave-thigh and the wave-breast shall they bring with the offerings made by fire of the fat, to wave it for a wave-offering before Jehovah: and it shall be thine, and thy sons' with thee, as a portion for ever; as Jehovah hath commanded. ASV

Leviticus 10:16

And Moses diligently sought the goat of the sin-offering, and, behold, it was burnt: and he was angry with Eleazar and with Ithamar, the sons of Aaron that were left, saying, ASV

Leviticus 10:17

Wherefore have ye not eaten the sin-offering in the place of the sanctuary, seeing it is most holy, and he hath given it you to bear the iniquity of the congregation, to make atonement for them before Jehovah? ASV

Leviticus 10:19

And Aaron spake unto Moses, Behold, this day have they offered their sin-offering and their burnt-offering before Jehovah; and there have befallen me such things as these: and if I had eaten the sin-offering to-day, would it have been well-pleasing in the sight of Jehovah? ASV

Leviticus 12:6

And when the days of her purifying are fulfilled, for a son, or for a daughter, she shall bring a lamb a year old for a burnt-offering, and a young pigeon, or a turtle-dove, for a sin-offering, unto the door of the tent of meeting, unto the priest: ASV

Leviticus 12:8

And if her means suffice not for a lamb, then she shall take two turtle-doves, or two young pigeons; the one for a burnt-offering, and the other for a sin-offering: and the priest shall make atonement for her, and she shall be clean. ASV

Leviticus 14:10

And on the eighth day he shall take two he-lambs without blemish, and one ewe-lamb a year old without blemish, and three tenth parts (of an ephah) of fine flour for a meal-offering, mingled with oil, and one log of oil. ASV

Leviticus 14:12

And the priest shall take one of the he-lambs, and offer him for a trespass-offering, and the log of oil, and wave them for a wave-offering before Jehovah: ASV

Leviticus 14:13

And he shall kill the he-lamb in the place where they kill the sin-offering and the burnt-offering, in the place of the sanctuary: for as the sin-offering is the priest's, so is the trespass-offering: it is most holy: ASV

Leviticus 14:14

And the priest shall take of the blood of the trespass-offering, and the priest shall put it upon the tip of the right ear of him that is to be cleansed, and upon the thumb of his right hand, and upon the great toe of his right foot. ASV

Leviticus 14:17

And of the rest of the oil that is in his hand shall the priest put upon the tip of the right ear of him that is to be cleansed, and upon the thumb of his right hand, and upon the great toe of his right foot, upon the blood of the trespass-offering: ASV

Leviticus 14:19

And the priest shall offer the sin-offering, and make atonement for him that is to be cleansed because of his uncleanness: and afterward he shall kill the burnt-offering; ASV

Leviticus 14:20

And the priest shall offer the burnt-offering and the meal-offering upon the altar: and the priest shall make atonement for him, and he shall be clean. ASV

Leviticus 14:21

And if he be poor, and cannot get so much, then he shall take one he-lamb for a trespass-offering to be waved, to make atonement for him, and one tenth part (of an ephah) of fine flour mingled with oil for a meal-offering, and a log of oil; ASV

Leviticus 14:22

And two turtle-doves, or two young pigeons, such as he is able to get; and the one shall be a sin-offering, and the other a burnt-offering. ASV

Leviticus 14:24

And the priest shall take the lamb of the trespass-offering, and the log of oil, and the priest shall wave them for a wave-offering before Jehovah. ASV

Leviticus 14:25

And he shall kill the lamb of the trespass-offering; and the priest shall take of the blood of the trespass-offering, and put it upon the tip of the right ear of him that is to be cleansed, and upon the thumb of his right hand, and upon the great toe of his right foot. ASV

Leviticus 14:28

And the priest shall put of the oil that is in his hand upon the tip of the right ear of him that is to be cleansed, and upon the thumb of his right hand, and upon the great toe of his right foot, upon the place of the blood of the trespass-offering: ASV

Leviticus 14:31

Even such as he is able to get, the one for a sin-offering, and the other for a burnt-offering, with the meal-offering: and the priest shall make atonement for him that is to be cleansed before Jehovah. ASV

Leviticus 15:15

And the priest shall offer them, the one for a sin-offering, and the other for a burnt-offering; and the priest shall make atonement for him before Jehovah for his issue. ASV

Leviticus 15:30

And the priest shall offer the one for a sin-offering, and the other for a burnt-offering; and the priest shall make atonement for her before Jehovah for the issue of her uncleanness. ASV

Leviticus 16:3

Herewith shall Aaron come into the holy place: with a young bullock for a sin-offering, and a ram for a burnt-offering. ASV

Leviticus 16:5

And he shall take of the congregation of the children of Israel two he-goats for a sin-offering, and one ram for a burnt-offering. ASV

Leviticus 16:6

And Aaron shall present the bullock of the sin-offering, which is for himself, and make atonement for himself, and for his house. ASV

Leviticus 16:9

And Aaron shall present the goat upon which the lot fell for Jehovah, and offer him for a sin-offering. ASV

Leviticus 16:11

And Aaron shall present the bullock of the sin-offering, which is for himself, and shall make atonement for himself, and for his house, and shall kill the bullock of the sin-offering which is for himself: ASV

Leviticus 16:15

Then shall he kill the goat of the sin-offering, that is for the people, and bring his blood within the veil, and do with his blood as he did with the blood of the bullock, and sprinkle it upon the mercy-seat, and before the mercy-seat: ASV

Leviticus 16:24

And he shall bathe his flesh in water in a holy place, and put on his garments, and come forth, and offer his burnt-offering and the burnt-offering of the people, and make atonement for himself and for the people. ASV

Leviticus 16:25

And the fat of the sin-offering shall he burn upon the altar. ASV

Leviticus 16:27

And the bullock of the sin-offering, and the goat of the sin-offering, whose blood was brought in to make atonement in the holy place, shall be carried forth without the camp; and they shall burn in the fire their skins, and their flesh, and their dung. ASV

Leviticus 17:4

And hath not brought it unto the door of the tent of meeting, to offer it as an oblation unto Jehovah before the tabernacle of Jehovah: blood shall be imputed unto that man; he hath shed blood; and that man shall be cut off from among his people: ASV

Leviticus 17:8

And thou shalt say unto them, Whatsoever man there be of the house of Israel, or of the strangers that sojourn among them, that offereth a burnt-offering or sacrifice, ASV

Leviticus 19:5

And when ye offer a sacrifice of peace-offerings unto Jehovah, ye shall offer it that ye may be accepted. ASV

Leviticus 19:21

And he shall bring his trespass-offering unto Jehovah, unto the door of the tent of meeting, even a ram for a trespass-offering. ASV

Leviticus 19:22

And the priest shall make atonement for him with the ram of the trespass-offering before Jehovah for his sin which he hath sinned: and the sin which he hath sinned shall be forgiven him. ASV

Leviticus 22:18

Speak unto Aaron, and to his sons, and unto all the children of Israel, and say unto them, Whosoever he be of the house of Israel, or of the sojourners in Israel, that offereth his oblation, whether it be any of their vows, or any of their freewill-offerings, which they offer unto Jehovah for a burnt-offering; ASV

Leviticus 22:21

And whosoever offereth a sacrifice of peace-offerings unto Jehovah to accomplish a vow, or for a freewill-offering, of the herd or of the flock, it shall be perfect to be accepted; there shall be no blemish therein. ASV

Leviticus 22:22

Blind, or broken, or maimed, or having a wen, or scurvy, or scabbed, ye shall not offer these unto Jehovah, nor make an offering by fire of them upon the altar unto Jehovah. ASV

Leviticus 22:23

Either a bullock or a lamb that hath anything superfluous or lacking in his parts, that mayest thou offer for a freewill-offering; but for a vow it shall not be accepted. ASV

Leviticus 22:24

That which hath its stones bruised, or crushed, or broken, or cut, ye shall not offer unto Jehovah; neither shall ye do (thus) in your land. ASV

Leviticus 22:27

When a bullock, or a sheep, or a goat, is brought forth, then it shall be seven days under the dam; and from the eighth day and thenceforth it shall be accepted for the oblation of an offering made by fire unto Jehovah. ASV

Leviticus 23:8

But ye shall offer an offering made by fire unto Jehovah seven days: in the seventh day is a holy convocation; ye shall do no servile work. ASV

Leviticus 23:12

And in the day when ye wave the sheaf, ye shall offer a he-lamb without blemish a year old for a burnt-offering unto Jehovah. ASV

Leviticus 23:13

And the meal-offering thereof shall be two tenth parts (of an ephah) of fine flour mingled with oil, an offering made by fire unto Jehovah for a sweet savor; and the drink-offering thereof shall be of wine, the fourth part of a hin. ASV

Leviticus 23:14

And ye shall eat neither bread, nor parched grain, nor fresh ears, until this selfsame day, until ye have brought the oblation of your God: it is a statute for ever throughout your generations in all your dwellings. ASV

Leviticus 23:15

And ye shall count unto you from the morrow after the sabbath, from the day that ye brought the sheaf of the wave-offering; seven sabbaths shall there be complete: ASV

Leviticus 23:16

Even unto the morrow after the seventh sabbath shall ye number fifty days; and ye shall offer a new meal-offering unto Jehovah. ASV

Leviticus 23:18

And ye shall present with the bread seven lambs without blemish a year old, and one young bullock, and two rams: they shall be a burnt-offering unto Jehovah, with their meal-offering, and their drink-offerings, even an offering made by fire, of a sweet savor unto Jehovah. ASV

Leviticus 23:19

And ye shall offer one he-goat for a sin-offering, and two he-lambs a year old for a sacrifice of peace-offerings. ASV

Leviticus 23:20

And the priest shall wave them with the bread of the first-fruits for a wave-offering before Jehovah, with the two lambs: they shall be holy to Jehovah for the priest. ASV

Leviticus 23:25

Ye shall do no servile work; and ye shall offer an offering made by fire unto Jehovah. ASV

Leviticus 23:27

Howbeit on the tenth day of this seventh month is the day of atonement: it shall be a holy convocation unto you, and ye shall afflict your souls; and ye shall offer an offering made by fire unto Jehovah. ASV

Leviticus 23:36

Seven days ye shall offer an offering made by fire unto Jehovah: on the eighth day shall be a holy convocation unto you; and ye shall offer an offering made by fire unto Jehovah: it is a solemn assembly; ye shall do no servile work. ASV

Leviticus 23:37

These are the set feasts of Jehovah, which ye shall proclaim to be holy convocations, to offer an offering made by fire unto Jehovah, a burnt-offering, and a meal-offering, a sacrifice, and drink-offerings, each on its own day; ASV

Leviticus 24:7

And thou shalt put pure frankincense upon each row, that it may be to the bread for a memorial, even an offering made by fire unto Jehovah. ASV

Leviticus 24:9

And it shall be for Aaron and his sons; and they shall eat it in a holy place: for it is most holy unto him of the offerings of Jehovah made by fire by a perpetual statute. ASV

Numbers 4:16

And the charge of Eleazar the son of Aaron the priest shall be the oil for the light, and the sweet incense, and the continual meal-offering, and the anointing oil, the charge of all the tabernacle, and of all that therein is, the sanctuary, and the furniture thereof. ASV

Numbers 5:9

And every heave-offering of all the holy things of the children of Israel, which they present unto the priest, shall be his. ASV

Numbers 5:15

Then shall the man bring his wife unto the priest, and shall bring her oblation for her, the tenth part of an ephah of barley meal; he shall pour no oil upon it, nor put frankincense thereon; for it is a meal-offering of jealousy, a meal-offering of memorial, bringing iniquity to remembrance. ASV

Numbers 5:18

And the priest shall set the woman before Jehovah, and let the hair of the woman's head go loose, and put the meal-offering of memorial in her hands, which is the meal-offering of jealousy: and the priest shall have in his hand the water of bitterness that causeth the curse. ASV

Numbers 5:25

And the priest shall take the meal-offering of jealousy out of the woman's hand, and shall wave the meal-offering before Jehovah, and bring it unto the altar: ASV

All the Financial Scriptures in the Bible with Commentary

Numbers 5:26

And the priest shall take a handful of the meal-offering, as the memorial thereof, and burn it upon the altar, and afterward shall make the woman drink the water. ASV

Numbers 6:11

And the priest shall offer one for a sin-offering, and the other for a burnt-offering, and make atonement for him, for that he sinned by reason of the dead, and shall hallow his head that same day. ASV

Numbers 6:12

And he shall separate unto Jehovah the days of his separation, and shall bring a he-lamb a year old for a trespass-offering; but the former days shall be void, because his separation was defiled. ASV

Numbers 6:14

And he shall offer his oblation unto Jehovah, one he-lamb a year old without blemish for a burnt-offering, and one ewe-lamb a year old without blemish for a sin-offering, and one ram without blemish for peace-offerings, ASV

Numbers 6:15

And a basket of unleavened bread, cakes of fine flour mingled with oil, and unleavened wafers anointed with oil, and their meal-offering, and their drink-offerings. ASV

Numbers 6:16

And the priest shall present them before Jehovah, and shall offer his sin-offering, and his burnt-offering: ASV

Numbers 6:17

And he shall offer the ram for a sacrifice of peace-offerings unto Jehovah, with the basket of unleavened bread: the priest shall offer also the meal-offering thereof, and the drink-offering thereof. ASV

Numbers 6:18

And the Nazirite shall shave the head of his separation at the door of the tent of meeting, and shall take the hair of the head of his separation, and put it on the fire which is under the sacrifice of peace-offerings. ASV

Numbers 6:20

And the priest shall wave them for a wave-offering before Jehovah; this is holy for the priest, together with the wave-breast and heave-thigh: and after that the Nazirite may drink wine. ASV

Numbers 6:21

This is the law of the Nazirite who voweth, (and of) his oblation unto Jehovah for his separation, besides that which he is able to get: according to his vow which he voweth, so he must do after the law of his separation. ASV

Numbers 7:3

And they brought their oblation before Jehovah, six covered wagons, and twelve oxen; a wagon for every two of the princes, and for each one an ox: and they presented them before the tabernacle. ASV

Numbers 7:10

And the princes offered for the dedication of the altar in the day that it was anointed, even the princes offered their oblation before the altar. ASV

Numbers 7:11

And Jehovah said unto Moses, They shall offer their oblation, each prince on his day, for the dedication of the altar. ASV

Numbers 7:12

And he that offered his oblation the first day was Nahshon the son of Amminadab, of the tribe of Judah: ASV

Numbers 7:13

And his oblation was one silver platter, the weight whereof was a hundred and thirty (shekels), one silver bowl of seventy shekels, after the shekel of the sanctuary; both of them full of fine flour mingled with oil for a meal-offering; ASV

Numbers 7:15

One young bullock, one ram, one he-lamb a year old, for a burnt-offering; ASV

Numbers 7:16

One male of the goats for a sin-offering; ASV

Numbers 7:17

And for the sacrifice of peace-offerings, two oxen, five rams, five he-goats, five he-lambs a year old: this was the oblation of Nahshon the son of Amminadab. ASV

Numbers 7:19

He offered for his oblation one silver platter, the weight whereof was a hundred and thirty (shekels), one silver bowl of seventy shekels, after the shekel of the sanctuary; both of them full of fine flour mingled with oil for a meal-offering; ASV

Numbers 7:20

One golden spoon of ten (shekels), full of incense; ASV

Numbers 7:21

One young bullock, one ram, one he-lamb a year old, for a burnt-offering; ASV

Numbers 7:22

One male of the goats for a sin-offering; ASV

Numbers 7:23

And for the sacrifice of peace-offerings, two oxen, five rams, five he-goats, five he-lambs a year old: this was the oblation of Nethanel the son of Zuar. ASV

Numbers 7:25

His oblation was one silver platter, the weight whereof was a hundred and thirty (shekels), one silver bowl of seventy shekels, after the shekel of the sanctuary; both of them full of fine flour mingled with oil for a meal-offering; ASV

Numbers 7:27

One young bullock, one ram, one he-lamb a year old, for a burnt-offering; ASV

Numbers 7:28

One male of the goats for a sin-offering; ASV

Numbers 7:29

And for the sacrifice of peace-offerings, two oxen, five rams, five he-goats, five he-lambs a year old: this was the oblation of Eliab the son of Helon. ASV

Numbers 7:31

His oblation was one silver platter, the weight whereof was a hundred and thirty (shekels), one silver bowl of seventy shekels, after the shekel of the sanctuary; both of them full of fine flour mingled with oil for a meal-offering; ASV

Numbers 7:33

One young bullock, one ram, one he-lamb a year old, for a burnt-offering; ASV

Numbers 7:34

One male of the goats for a sin-offering; ASV

Numbers 7:35

And for the sacrifice of peace-offerings, two oxen, five rams, five he-goats, five he-lambs a year old: this was the oblation of Elizur the son of Shedeur. ASV

Numbers 7:37

His oblation was one silver platter, the weight whereof was a hundred and thirty (shekels), one silver bowl of seventy shekels, after the shekel of the sanctuary; both of them full of fine flour mingled with oil for a meal-offering; ASV

Numbers 7:39

One young bullock, one ram, one he-lamb a year old, for a burnt-offering; ASV

Numbers 7:40

One male of the goats for a sin-offering; ASV

Numbers 7:41

And for the sacrifice of peace-offerings, two oxen, five rams, five he-goats, five he-lambs a year old: this was the oblation of Shelumiel the son of Zurishaddai. ASV

Numbers 7:43

His oblation was one silver platter, the weight whereof was a hundred and thirty (shekels), one silver bowl of seventy shekels, after the shekel of the sanctuary; both of them full of fine flour mingled with oil for a meal-offering; ASV

Numbers 7:45

One young bullock, one ram, one he-lamb a year old, for a burnt-offering; ASV

Numbers 7:46

One male of the goats for a sin-offering; ASV

Numbers 7:47

And for the sacrifice of peace-offerings, two oxen, five rams, five he-goats, five he-lambs a year old: this was the oblation of Eliasaph the son of Deuel. ASV

Numbers 7:49

His oblation was one silver platter, the weight whereof was a hundred and thirty (shekels), one silver bowl of seventy shekels, after the shekel of the sanctuary; both of them full of fine flour mingled with oil for a meal-offering; ASV

Numbers 7:51

One young bullock, one ram, one he-lamb a year old, for a burnt-offering; ASV

Numbers 7:52

One male of the goats for a sin-offering; ASV

Numbers 7:53

And for the sacrifice of peace-offerings, two oxen, five rams, five he-goats, five he-lambs a year old: this was the oblation of Elishama the son of Ammihud. ASV

Numbers 7:55

His oblation was one silver platter, the weight whereof was a hundred and thirty (shekels), one silver bowl of seventy shekels, after the shekel of the sanctuary; both of them full of fine flour mingled with oil for a meal-offering; ASV

Numbers 7:57

One young bullock, one ram, one he-lamb a year old, for a burnt-offering; ASV

Numbers 7:58

One male of the goats for a sin-offering; ASV

Numbers 7:59

And for the sacrifice of peace-offerings, two oxen, five rams, five he-goats, five he-lambs a year old: this was the oblation of Gamaliel the son of Pedahzur. ASV

Numbers 7:61

His oblation was one silver platter, the weight whereof was a hundred and thirty (shekels), one silver bowl of seventy shekels, after the shekel of the sanctuary; both of them full of fine flour mingled with oil for a meal-offering; ASV

Numbers 7:63

One young bullock, one ram, one he-lamb a year old, for a burnt-offering; ASV

Numbers 7:64

One male of the goats for a sin-offering; ASV

Numbers 7:65

And for the sacrifice of peace-offerings, two oxen, five rams, five he-goats, five he-lambs a year old: this was the oblation of Abidan the son of Gideoni. ASV

Numbers 7:67

His oblation was one silver platter, the weight whereof was a hundred and thirty (shekels), one silver bowl of seventy shekels, after the shekel of the sanctuary; both of them full of fine flour mingled with oil for a meal-offering; ASV

Numbers 7:69

One young bullock, one ram, one he-lamb a year old, for a burnt-offering; ASV

Numbers 7:70

One male of the goats for a sin-offering; ASV

Numbers 7:71

And for the sacrifice of peace-offerings, two oxen, five rams, five he-goats, five he-lambs a year old: this was the oblation of Ahiezer the son of Ammishaddai. ASV

Numbers 7:73

His oblation was one silver platter, the weight whereof was a hundred and thirty (shekels), one silver bowl of seventy shekels, after the shekel of the sanctuary; both of them full of fine flour mingled with oil for a meal-offering; ASV

Numbers 7:75

One young bullock, one ram, one he-lamb a year old, for a burnt-offering; ASV

Numbers 7:76

One male of the goats for a sin-offering; ASV

Numbers 7:77

And for the sacrifice of peace-offerings, two oxen, five rams, five he-goats, five he-lambs a year old: this was the oblation of Pagiel the son of Ochran. ASV

Numbers 7:79

His oblation was one silver platter, the weight whereof was a hundred a thirty (shekels), one silver bowl of seventy shekels, after the shekel of the sanctuary; both of them full of fine flour mingled with oil for a meal-offering; ASV

Numbers 7:81

One young bullock, one ram, one he-lamb a year old, for a burnt-offering; ASV

Numbers 7:82

One male of the goats for a sin-offering; ASV

Numbers 7:83

And for the sacrifice of peace-offerings, two oxen, five rams, five he-goats, five he-lambs a year old: this was the oblation of Ahira the son of Enan. ASV

Numbers 7:87

All the oxen for the burnt-offering twelve bullocks, the rams twelve, the he-lambs a year old twelve, and their meal-offering; and the males of the goats for a sin-offering twelve; ASV

Numbers 7:88

And all the oxen for the sacrifice of peace-offerings twenty and four bullocks, the rams sixty, the he-goats sixty, the he-lambs a year old sixty. This was the dedication of the altar, after that it was anointed. ASV

Numbers 8:8

Then let them take a young bullock, and its meal-offering, fine flour mingled with oil; and another young bullock shalt thou take for a sin-offering. ASV

Numbers 8:11

And Aaron shall offer the Levites before Jehovah for a wave-offering, on the behalf of the children of Israel, that it may be theirs to do the service of Jehovah. ASV

Numbers 8:12

And the Levites shall lay their hands upon the heads of the bullocks: and offer thou the one for a sin-offering, and the other for a burnt-offering, unto Jehovah, to make atonement for the Levites. ASV

Numbers 8:13

And thou shalt set the Levites before Aaron, and before his sons, and offer them for a wave-offering unto Jehovah. ASV

Numbers 8:15

And after that shall the Levites go in to do the service of the tent of meeting: and thou shalt cleanse them, and offer them for a wave-offering. ASV

Numbers 8:21

And the Levites purified themselves from sin, and they washed their clothes: and Aaron offered them for a wave-offering before Jehovah; and Aaron made atonement for them to cleanse them. ASV

Numbers 9:7

And those men said unto him, We are unclean by reason of the dead body of a man: wherefore are we kept back, that we may not offer the oblation of Jehovah in its appointed season among the children of Israel? ASV

Numbers 9:13

But the man that is clean, and is not on a journey, and forbeareth to keep the passover, that soul shall be cut off from his people; because he offered not the oblation of Jehovah in its appointed season, that man shall bear his sin. ASV

Numbers 15:3

And will make an offering by fire unto Jehovah, a burnt-offering, or a sacrifice, to accomplish a vow, or as a freewill-offering, or in your set feasts, to make a sweet savor unto Jehovah, of the herd, or of the flock; ASV

Numbers 15:4

Then shall he that offereth his oblation offer unto Jehovah a meal-offering of a tenth part (of an ephah) of fine flour mingled with the fourth part of a hin of oil: ASV

Numbers 15:5

And wine for the drink-offering, the fourth part of a hin, shalt thou prepare with the burnt-offering, or for the sacrifice, for each lamb. ASV

Numbers 15:6

Or for a ram, thou shalt prepare for a meal-offering two tenth parts (of an ephah) of fine flour mingled with the third part of a hin of oil: ASV

Numbers 15:7

And for the drink-offering thou shalt offer the third part of a hin of wine, of a sweet savor unto Jehovah. ASV

Numbers 15:8

And when thou preparest a bullock for a burnt-offering, or for a sacrifice, to accomplish a vow, or for peace-offerings unto Jehovah; ASV

Numbers 15:9

Then shall he offer with the bullock a meal-offering of three tenth parts (of an ephah) of fine flour mingled with half a hin of oil: ASV

Numbers 15:10

And thou shalt offer for the drink-offering half a hin of wine, for an offering made by fire, of a sweet savor unto Jehovah. ASV

Numbers 15:13

All that are home-born shall do these things after this manner, in offering an offering made by fire, of a sweet savor unto Jehovah. ASV

Numbers 15:14

And if a stranger sojourn with you, or whosoever may be among you throughout your generations, and will offer an offering made by fire, of a sweet savor unto Jehovah; as ye do, so he shall do. ASV

Numbers 15:19

Then it shall be, that, when ye eat of the bread of the land, ye shall offer up a heave-offering unto Jehovah. ASV

Numbers 15:20

Of the first of your dough ye shall offer up a cake for a heave-offering: as the heave-offering of the threshing-floor, so shall ye heave it. ASV

Numbers 15:21

Of the first of your dough ye shall give unto Jehovah a heave-offering throughout your generations. ASV

Numbers 15:24

Then it shall be, if it be done unwittingly, without the knowledge of the congregation, that all the congregation shall offer one young bullock for a burnt-offering, for a sweet savor unto Jehovah, with the meal-offering thereof, and the drink-offering thereof, according to the ordinance, and one he-goat for a sin-offering. ASV

Numbers 15:25

And the priest shall make atonement for all the congregation of the children of Israel, and they shall be forgiven; for it was an error, and they have brought their oblation, an offering made by fire unto Jehovah, and their sin-offering before Jehovah, for their error: ASV

Numbers 15:27

And if one person sin unwittingly, then he shall offer a she-goat a year old for a sin-offering. ASV

Numbers 16:15

And Moses was very wroth, and said unto Jehovah, Respect not thou their offering: I have not taken one ass from them, neither have I hurt one of them. ASV

Numbers 18:9

This shall be thine of the most holy things, (reserved) from the fire: every oblation of theirs, even every meal-offering of theirs, and every sin-offering of theirs, and every trespass-offering of theirs, which they shall render unto me, shall be most holy for thee and for thy sons. ASV

Numbers 18:11

And this is thine: the heave-offering of their gift, even all the wave-offerings of the children of Israel; I have given them unto thee, and to thy sons and to thy daughters with thee, as a portion for ever; every one that is clean in thy house shall eat thereof. ASV

Numbers 18:17

But the firstling of a cow, or the firstling of a sheep, or the firstling of a goat, thou shalt not redeem; they are holy: thou shalt sprinkle their blood upon the altar, and shalt burn their fat for an offering made by fire, for a sweet savor unto Jehovah. ASV

Numbers 18:24

For the tithe of the children of Israel, which they offer as a heave-offering unto Jehovah, I have given to the Levites for an inheritance: therefore I have said unto them, Among the children of Israel they shall have no inheritance. ASV

Numbers 18:26

Moreover thou shalt speak unto the Levites, and say unto them, When ye take of the children of Israel the tithe which I have given you from them for your inheritance, then ye shall offer up a heave-offering of it for Jehovah, a tithe of the tithe. ASV

Numbers 18:27

And your heave-offering shall be reckoned unto you, as though it were the grain of the threshing-floor, and as the fulness of the winepress. ASV

Numbers 18:28

Thus ye also shall offer a heave-offering unto Jehovah of all your tithes, which ye receive of the children of Israel; and thereof ye shall give Jehovah's heave-offering to Aaron the priest. ASV

Numbers 18:29

Out of all your gifts ye shall offer every heave-offering of Jehovah, of all the best thereof, even the hallowed part thereof out of it. ASV

Numbers 23:3

And Balaam said unto Balak, Stand by thy burnt-offering, and I will go: peradventure Jehovah will come to meet me; and whatsoever he showeth me I will tell thee. And he went to a bare height. ASV

Numbers 23:15

And he said unto Balak, Stand here by thy burnt-offering, while I meet (Jehovah) yonder. ASV

Numbers 23:17

And he came to him, and, lo, he was standing by his burnt-offering, and the princes of Moab with him. And Balak said unto him, What hath Jehovah spoken? ASV

Numbers 28:2

Command the children of Israel, and say unto them, My oblation, my food for my offerings made by fire, of a sweet savor unto me, shall ye observe to offer unto me in their due season. ASV

Numbers 28:3

And thou shalt say unto them, This is the offering made by fire which ye shall offer unto Jehovah: he-lambs a year old without blemish, two day by day, for a continual burnt-offering. ASV

Numbers 28:5

And the tenth part of an ephah of fine flour for a meal-offering, mingled with the fourth part of a hin of beaten oil. ASV

Numbers 28:6

It is a continual burnt-offering, which was ordained in mount Sinai for a sweet savor, an offering made by fire unto Jehovah. ASV

Numbers 28:7

And the drink-offering thereof shall be the fourth part of a hin for the one lamb: in the holy place shalt thou pour out a drink-offering of strong drink unto Jehovah. ASV

Numbers 28:8

And the other lamb shalt thou offer at even: as the meal-offering of the morning, and as the drink-offering thereof, thou shalt offer it, an offering made by fire, of a sweet savor unto Jehovah. ASV

Numbers 28:9

And on the sabbath day two he-lambs a year old without blemish, and two tenth parts (of an ephah) of fine flour for a meal-offering, mingled with oil, and the drink-offering thereof: ASV

Numbers 28:10

This is the burnt-offering of every sabbath, besides the continual burnt-offering, and the drinkoffering thereof. ASV

Numbers 28:11

And in the beginnings of your months ye shall offer a burnt-offering unto Jehovah: two young bullocks, and one ram, seven he-lambs a year old without blemish; ASV

Numbers 28:12

And three tenth parts (of an ephah) of fine flour for a meal-offering, mingled with oil, for each bullock; and two tenth parts of fine flour for a meal-offering, mingled with oil, for the one ram; ASV

Numbers 28:13

And a tenth part of fine flour mingled with oil for a meal-offering unto every lamb; for a burnt-offering of a sweet savor, an offering made by fire unto Jehovah. ASV

Numbers 28:14

And their drink-offerings shall be half a hin of wine for a bullock, and the third part of a hin for the ram, and the fourth part of a hin for a lamb: this is the burnt-offering of every month throughout the months of the year. ASV

Numbers 28:15

And one he-goat for a sin-offering unto Jehovah; it shall be offered besides the continual burnt-offering, and the drink-offering thereof. ASV

Numbers 28:16

And in the first month, on the fourteenth day of the month, is Jehovah's passover. ASV

Numbers 28:17

And on the fifteenth day of this month shall be a feast: seven days shall unleavened bread be eaten. ASV

Numbers 28:18

In the first day shall be a holy convocation: ye shall do no servile work; ASV

Numbers 28:19

But ye shall offer an offering made by fire, a burnt-offering unto Jehovah: two young bullocks, and one ram, and seven he-lambs a year old; they shall be unto you without blemish; ASV

Numbers 28:20

And their meal-offering, fine flour mingled with oil: three tenth parts shall ye offer for a bullock, and two tenth parts for the ram; ASV

Numbers 28:22

And one he-goat for a sin-offering, to make atonement for you. ASV

Numbers 28:23

Ye shall offer these besides the burnt-offering of the morning, which is for a continual burnt-offering. ASV

Numbers 28:24

After this manner ye shall offer daily, for seven days, the food of the offering made by fire, of a sweet savor unto Jehovah: it shall be offered besides the continual burnt-offering, and the drink-offering thereof. ASV

Numbers 28:26

Also in the day of the first-fruits, when ye offer a new meal-offering unto Jehovah in your (feast of) weeks, ye shall have a holy convocation; ye shall do no servile work; ASV

Numbers 28:27

But ye shall offer a burnt-offering for a sweet savor unto Jehovah: two young bullocks, one ram, seven he-lambs a year old; ASV

Numbers 28:28

And their meal-offering, fine flour mingled with oil, three tenth parts for each bullock, two tenth parts for the one ram, ASV

Numbers 28:31

Besides the continual burnt-offering, and the meal-offering thereof, ye shall offer them (they shall be unto you without blemish), and their drink-offerings. ASV

Numbers 29:2

And ye shall offer a burnt-offering for a sweet savor unto Jehovah: one young bullock, one ram, seven he-lambs a year old without blemish; ASV

Numbers 29:3

And their meal-offering, fine flour mingled with oil, three tenth parts for the bullock, two tenth parts for the ram, ASV

Numbers 29:5

And one he-goat for a sin-offering, to make atonement for you; ASV

Numbers 29:6

Besides the burnt-offering of the new moon, and the meal-offering thereof, and the continual burnt-offering and the meal-offering thereof, and their drink-offerings, according unto their ordinance, for a sweet savor, an offering made by fire unto Jehovah. ASV

Numbers 29:8

But ye shall offer a burnt-offering unto Jehovah for a sweet savor: one young bullock, one ram, seven he-lambs a year old; they shall be unto you without blemish; ASV

Numbers 29:9

And their meal-offering, fine flour mingled with oil, three tenth parts for the bullock, two tenth parts for the one ram, ASV

Numbers 29:11

One he-goat for a sin-offering; besides the sin-offering of atonement, and the continual burnt-offering, and the meal-offering thereof, and their drink-offerings. ASV

Numbers 29:13

And ye shall offer a burnt-offering, an offering made by fire, of a sweet savor unto Jehovah; thirteen young bullocks, two rams, fourteen he-lambs a year old; they shall be without blemish; ASV

Numbers 29:14

And their meal-offering, fine flour mingled with oil, three tenth parts for every bullock of the thirteen bullocks, two tenth parts for each ram of the two rams, ASV

Numbers 29:16

And one he-goat for a sin-offering, besides the continual burnt-offering, the meal-offering thereof, and the drink-offering thereof. ASV

Numbers 29:18

And their meal-offering and their drink-offerings for the bullocks, for the rams, and for the lambs, according to their number, after the ordinance; ASV

Numbers 29:19

And one he-goat for a sin-offering; besides the continual burnt-offering, and the meal-offering thereof, and their drink-offerings. ASV

Numbers 29:21

And their meal-offering and their drink-offerings for the bullocks, for the rams, and for the lambs, according to their number, after the ordinance; ASV

Numbers 29:22

And one he-goat for a sin-offering; besides the continual burnt-offering, and the meal-offering thereof, and the drink-offering thereof. ASV

Numbers 29:24

Their meal-offering and their drink-offerings for the bullocks, for the rams, and for the lambs, according to their number, after the ordinance; ASV

Numbers 29:25

And one he-goat for a sin-offering; besides the continual burnt-offering, the meal-offering thereof, and the drink-offering thereof. ASV

Numbers 29:27

And their meal-offering and their drink-offerings for the bullocks, for the rams, and for the lambs, according to their number, after the ordinance; ASV

Numbers 29:28

And one he-goat for a sin-offering, besides the continual burnt-offering, and the meal-offering thereof, and the drink-offering thereof. ASV

Numbers 29:30

And their meal-offering and their drink-offerings for the bullocks, for the rams, and for the lambs, according to their number, after the ordinance; ASV

Numbers 29:31

And one he-goat for a sin-offering; besides the continual burnt-offering, the meal-offering thereof, and the drink-offerings thereof. ASV

Numbers 29:33

And their meal-offering and their drink-offerings for the bullocks, for the rams, and for the lambs, according to their number, after the ordinance; ASV

Numbers 29:34

And one he-goat for a sin-offering; besides the continual burnt-offering, the meal-offering thereof, and the drink-offering thereof. ASV

Numbers 29:36

But ye shall offer a burnt-offering, an offering made by fire, of a sweet savor unto Jehovah: one bullock, one ram, seven he-lambs a year old without blemish; ASV

Numbers 29:37

Their meal-offering and their drink-offerings for the bullock, for the ram, and for the lambs, shall be according to their number, after the ordinance: ASV

All the Financial Scriptures in the Bible with Commentary

Numbers 29:38

And one he-goat for a sin-offering, besides the continual burnt-offering, and the meal-offering thereof, and the drink-offering thereof. ASV

Numbers 31:29

Take it of their half, and give it unto Eleazar the priest, for Jehovah's heave-offering. ASV

Numbers 31:41

And Moses gave the tribute, which was Jehovah's heave-offering, unto Eleazar the priest, as Jehovah commanded Moses. ASV

Numbers 31:52

And all the gold of the heave-offering that they offered up to Jehovah, of the captains of thousands, and of the captains of hundreds, was sixteen thousand seven hundred and fifty shekels. ASV

Deuteronomy 12:17

Thou mayest not eat within thy gates the tithe of thy grain, or of thy new wine, or of thine oil, or the firstlings of thy herd or of thy flock, nor any of thy vows which thou vow-

est, nor thy freewill-offerings, nor the heave-offering of thy hand; ASV

Deuteronomy 16:10

And thou shalt keep the feast of weeks unto Jehovah thy God with a tribute of a freewill-offering of thy hand, which thou shalt give, according as Jehovah thy God blesseth thee: ASV

Deuteronomy 23:23

That which is gone out of thy lips thou shalt observe and do; according as thou hast vowed unto Jehovah thy God, a freewill-offering, which thou hast promised with thy mouth. ASV

Deuteronomy 32:38

Which did eat the fat of their sacrifices, (And) drank the wine of their drink-offering? Let them rise up and help you, Let them be your protection. ASV

Joshua 22:26

Therefore we said, Let us now prepare to build us an altar, not for burnt-offering, nor for sacrifice: ASV

Judges 11:31

Then it shall be, that whatsoever cometh forth from the doors of my house to meet me, when I return in peace from

the children of Ammon, it shall be Jehovah's, and I will offer it up for a burnt-offering. ASV

Judges 13:16

And the angel of Jehovah said unto Manoah, Though thou detain me, I will not eat of thy bread; and if thou wilt make ready a burnt-offering, thou must offer it unto Jehovah. For Manoah knew not that he was the angel of Jehovah. ASV

Judges 13:19

So Manoah took the kid with the meal-offering, and offered it upon the rock unto Jehovah: and (the angel) did wondrously, and Manoah and his wife looked on. ASV

Judges 13:23

But his wife said unto him, If Jehovah were pleased to kill us, he would not have received a burnt-offering and a meal-offering at our hand, neither would he have showed us all these things, nor would at this time have told such things as these. ASV

1 Samuel 2:17

And the sin of the young men was very great before Jehovah; for the men despised the offering of Jehovah. ASV

1 Samuel 2:29

Wherefore kick ye at my sacrifice and at mine offering, which I have commanded in (my) habitation, and honorest thy sons above me, to make yourselves fat with the chiefest of all the offerings of Israel my people? ASV

1 Samuel 3:14

And therefore I have sworn unto the house of Eli, that the iniquity of Eli's house shall not be expiated with sacrifice nor offering for ever. ASV

1 Samuel 6:3

And they said, If ye send away the ark of the God of Israel, send it not empty; but by all means return him a trespass-offering: then ye shall be healed, and it shall be known to you why his hand is not removed from you. ASV

1 Samuel 6:4

Then said they, What shall be the trespass-offering which we shall return to him? And they said, Five golden tumors, and five golden mice, (according to) the number of the lords of the Philistines; for one plague was on you all, and on your lords. ASV

1 Samuel 6:8

And take the ark of Jehovah, and lay it upon the cart; and put the jewels of gold, which ye return him for a trespass-offering, in a coffer by the side thereof; and send it away, that it may go. ASV

1 Samuel 6:14

And the cart came into the field of Joshua the Beth-shemite, and stood there, where there was a great stone: and they clave the wood of the cart, and offered up the kine for a burnt-offering unto Jehovah. ASV

1 Samuel 6:17

And these are the golden tumors which the Philistines returned for a trespass-offering unto Jehovah: for Ashdod one, for Gaza one, for Ashkelon one, for Gath one, for Ekron one; ASV

1 Samuel 7:9

And Samuel took a sucking lamb, and offered it for a whole burnt-offering unto Jehovah: and Samuel cried unto Jehovah for Israel; and Jehovah answered him. ASV

1 Samuel 7:10

And as Samuel was offering up the burnt-offering, the Philistines drew near to battle against Israel; but Jehovah thun-

dered with a great thunder on that day upon the Philistines, and discomfited them; and they were smitten down before Israel. ASV

1 Samuel 13:9

And Saul said, Bring hither the burnt-offering to me, and the peace-offerings. And he offered the burnt-offering. ASV

1 Samuel 13:10

And it came to pass that, as soon as he had made an end of offering the burnt-offering, behold, Samuel came; and Saul went out to meet him, that he might salute him. ASV

1 Samuel 13:12

Therefore said I, Now will the Philistines come down upon me to Gilgal, and I have not entreated the favor of Jehovah: I forced myself therefore, and offered the burnt-offering. ASV

1 Samuel 26:19

Now therefore, I pray thee, let my lord the king hear the words of his servant. If it be Jehovah that hath stirred thee up against me, let him accept an offering: but if it be the children of men, cursed be they before Jehovah: for they have driven me out this day that I should not cleave unto the inheritance of Jehovah, saying, Go, serve other gods. ASV

All the Financial Scriptures in the Bible with Commentary

2 Samuel 6:18

And when David had made an end of offering the burnt-offering and the peace-offerings, he blessed the people in the name of Jehovah of hosts. ASV

1 Kings 18:29

And it was so, when midday was past, that they prophesied until the time of the offering of the (evening) oblation; but there was neither voice, nor any to answer, nor any that regarded. ASV

1 Kings 18:36

And it came to pass at the time of the offering of the (evening) oblation, that Elijah the prophet came near, and said, O Jehovah, the God of Abraham, of Isaac, and of Israel, let it be known this day that thou art God in Israel, and that I am thy servant, and that I have done all these things at thy word. ASV

2 Kings 3:20

And it came to pass in the morning, about the time of offering the oblation, that, behold, there came water by the way of Edom, and the country was filled with water. ASV

2 Kings 3:27

Then he took his eldest son that should have reigned in his stead, and offered him for a burnt-offering upon the wall. And there was great wrath against Israel: and they departed from him, and returned to their own land. ASV

2 Kings 5:17

And Naaman said, If not, yet, I pray thee, let there be given to thy servant two mules' burden of earth; for thy servant will henceforth offer neither burnt-offering nor sacrifice unto other gods, but unto Jehovah. ASV

2 Kings 10:25

And it came to pass, as soon as he had made an end of offering the burnt-offering, that Jehu said to the guard and to the captains, Go in, and slay them; let none come forth. And they smote them with the edge of the sword; and the guard and the captains cast them out, and went to the city of the house of Baal. ASV

2 Kings 16:13

And he burnt his burnt-offering and his meal-offering, and poured his drink-offering, and sprinkled the blood of his peace-offerings, upon the altar. ASV

2 Kings 16:15

And king Ahaz commanded Urijah the priest, saying, Upon the great altar burn the morning burnt-offering, and the evening meal-offering, and the king's burnt-offering, and his meal-offering, with the burnt-offering of all the people of the land, and their meal-offering, and their drink-offerings; and sprinkle upon it all the blood of the burnt-offering, and all the blood of the sacrifice: but the brazen altar shall be for me to inquire by. ASV

1 Chronicles 6:49-50

But Aaron and his sons offered upon the altar of burnt-offering, and upon the altar of incense, for all the work of the most holy place, and to make atonement for Israel, according to all that Moses the servant of God had commanded. And these are the sons of Aaron: Eleazar his son, Phinehas his son, Abishua his son, ASV

1 Chronicles 16:2

And when David had made an end of offering the burnt-offering and the peace-offerings, he blessed the people in the name of Jehovah. ASV

1 Chronicles 16:29

Ascribe unto Jehovah the glory due unto his name: Bring an offering, and come before him: Worship Jehovah in holy array. ASV

1 Chronicles 16:40

To offer burnt-offerings unto Jehovah upon the altar of burnt-offering continually morning and evening, even according to all that is written in the law of Jehovah, which he commanded unto Israel; ASV

1 Chronicles 21:23

And Ornan said unto David, Take it to thee, and let my lord the king do that which is good in his eyes: lo, I give (thee) the oxen for burnt-offerings, and the threshing instruments for wood, and the wheat for the meal-offering; I give it all. ASV

1 Chronicles 21:26

And David built there an altar unto Jehovah, and offered burnt-offerings and peace-offerings, and called upon Jehovah; and he answered him from heaven by fire upon the altar of burnt-offering. ASV

1 Chronicles 21:29

For the tabernacle of Jehovah, which Moses made in the wilderness, and the altar of burnt-offering, were at that time in the high place at Gibeon. ASV

1 Chronicles 22:1

Then David said, This is the house of Jehovah God, and this is the altar of burnt-offering for Israel. ASV

1 Chronicles 23:29

For the showbread also, and for the fine flour for a meal-offering, whether of unleavened wafers, or of that which is baked in the pan, or of that which is soaked, and for all manner of measure and size; ASV

2 Chronicles 4:6

He made also ten lavers, and put five on the right hand, and five on the left, to wash in them; such things as belonged to the burnt-offering they washed in them; but the sea was for the priests to wash in. ASV

2 Chronicles 7:1

Now when Solomon had made an end of praying, the fire came down from heaven, and consumed the burnt-offering and the sacrifices; and the glory of Jehovah filled the house. ASV

2 Chronicles 8:13

Even as the duty of every day required, offering according to the commandment of Moses, on the sabbaths, and on the new moons, and on the set feasts, three times in the year, (even) in the feast of unleavened bread, and in the feast of weeks, and in the feast of tabernacles. ASV

2 Chronicles 24:14

And when they had made an end, they brought the rest of the money before the king and Jehoiada, whereof were made vessels for the house of Jehovah, even vessels wherewith to minister and to offer, and spoons, and vessels of gold and silver. And they offered burnt-offerings in the house of Jehovah continually all the days of Jehoiada. ASV

2 Chronicles 29:21

And they brought seven bullocks, and seven rams, and seven lambs, and seven he-goats, for a sin-offering for the kingdom and for the sanctuary and for Judah. And he commanded the priests the sons of Aaron to offer them on the altar of Jehovah. ASV

2 Chronicles 29:23

And they brought near the he-goats for the sin-offering before the king and the assembly; and they laid their hands upon them: ASV

2 Chronicles 29:24

And the priests killed them, and they made a sin-offering with their blood upon the altar, to make atonement for all Israel; for the king commanded (that) the burnt-offering and the sin-offering (should be made) for all Israel. ASV

2 Chronicles 29:27

And Hezekiah commanded to offer the burnt-offering upon the altar. And when the burnt-offering began, the song of Jehovah began also, and the trumpets, together with the instruments of David king of Israel. ASV

2 Chronicles 29:28

And all the assembly worshipped, and the singers sang, and the trumpeters sounded; all this (continued) until the burnt-offering was finished. ASV

2 Chronicles 29:29

And when they had made an end of offering, the king and all that were present with him bowed themselves and worshipped. ASV

2 Chronicles 29:32

And the number of the burnt-offerings which the assembly brought was threescore and ten bullocks, a hundred rams, and two hundred lambs: all these were for a burnt-offering to Jehovah. ASV

2 Chronicles 29:35

And also the burnt-offerings were in abundance, with the fat of the peace-offerings, and with the drink-offerings for every burnt-offering. So the service of the house of Jehovah was set in order. ASV

2 Chronicles 30:22

And Hezekiah spake comfortably unto all the Levites that had good understanding (in the service) of Jehovah. So they did eat throughout the feast for the seven days, offering sacrifices of peace-offerings, and making confession to Jehovah, the God of their fathers. ASV

2 Chronicles 35:14

And afterward they prepared for themselves, and for the priests, because the priests the sons of Aaron (were busied) in offering the burnt-offerings and the fat until night: therefore the Levites prepared for themselves, and for the priests the sons of Aaron. ASV

Ezra 3:5

And afterward the continual burnt-offering, and (the offerings) of the new moons, and of all the set feasts of Jehovah that were consecrated, and of every one that willingly offered a freewill-offering unto Jehovah. ASV

Ezra 6:17

And they offered at the dedication of this house of God a hundred bullocks, two hundred rams, four hundred lambs; and for a sin-offering for all Israel, twelve he-goats, according to the number of the tribes of Israel. ASV

Ezra 7:16

And all the silver and gold that thou shalt find in all the province of Babylon, with the freewill-offering of the people, and of the priests, offering willingly for the house of their God which is in Jerusalem; ASV

Ezra 8:25

And weighed unto them the silver, and the gold, and the vessels, even the offering for the house of our God, which the king, and his counsellors, and his princes, and all Israel there present, had offered: ASV

Ezra 8:28

And I said unto them, Ye are holy unto Jehovah, and the vessels are holy; and the silver and the gold are a freewill-offering unto Jehovah, the God of your fathers. ASV

Ezra 8:35

The children of the captivity, that were come out of exile, offered burnt-offerings unto the God of Israel, twelve bullocks for all Israel, ninety and six rams, seventy and seven lambs, twelve he-goats for a sin-offering: all this was a burnt-offering unto Jehovah. ASV

Nehemiah 10:33

For the showbread, and for the continual meal-offering, and for the continual burnt-offering, for the sabbaths, for the new moons, for the set feasts, and for the holy things, and for the sin-offerings to make atonement for Israel, and for all the work of the house of our God. ASV

Nehemiah 10:34

And we cast lots, the priests, the Levites, and the people, for the wood-offering, to bring it into the house of our God, according to our fathers' houses, at times appointed, year by year, to burn upon the altar of Jehovah our God, as it is written in the law; ASV

Nehemiah 10:39

For the children of Israel and the children of Levi shall bring the heave-offering of the grain, of the new wine, and of the oil, unto the chambers, where are the vessels of the sanctuary, and the priests that minister, and the porters, and the singers: and we will not forsake the house of our God. ASV

Nehemiah 13:9

Then I commanded, and they cleansed the chambers: and thither brought I again the vessels of the house of God, with the meal-offerings and the frankincense. ASV

Nehemiah 13:31

And for the wood-offering, at times appointed, and for the first-fruits. Remember me, O my God, for good. ASV

Job 42:8

Now therefore, take unto you seven bullocks and seven rams, and go to my servant Job, and offer up for yourselves a burnt-offering; and my servant Job shall pray for you; for him will I accept, that I deal not with you after your folly; for ye have not spoken of me the thing that is right, as my servant Job hath. ASV

Psalms 40:6

Sacrifice and offering thou hast no delight in; Mine ears hast thou opened: Burnt-offering and sin-offering hast thou not required. ASV

Psalms 51:16

For thou delightest not in sacrifice; else would I give it: Thou hast no pleasure in burnt-offering. ASV

Psalms 51:19

Then will thou delight in the sacrifices of righteousness, in burnt-offering and in whole burnt-offering: then will they offer bullocks upon thine altar. ASV

Psalms 96:8

Ascribe unto Jehovah the glory due unto his name: bring an offering, and come into his courts. ASV

Isaiah 40:16

And Lebanon is not sufficient to burn, nor the beasts thereof sufficient for a burnt-offering. ASV

Isaiah 53:10

Yet it pleased Jehovah to bruise him; he hath put him to grief: when thou shalt make his soul an offering for sin, he shall see (his) seed, he shall prolong his days, and the pleasure of Jehovah shall prosper in his hand. ASV

Isaiah 57:6

Among the smooth (stones) of the valley is thy portion; they, they are thy lot; even to them hast thou poured a drink-offering, thou hast offered an oblation. Shall I be appeased for these things? ASV

Isaiah 61:8

For I, Jehovah, love justice, I hate robbery with iniquity; and I will give them their recompense in truth, and I will make an everlasting covenant with them. ASV

Isaiah 65:11

But ye that forsake Jehovah, that forget my holy mountain, that prepare a table for Fortune, and that fill up mingled wine unto Destiny; ASV

Isaiah 66:20

And they shall bring all your brethren out of all the nations for an oblation unto Jehovah, upon horses, and in chariots, and in litters, and upon mules, and upon dromedaries, to my holy mountain Jerusalem, saith Jehovah, as the children of Israel bring their oblation in a clean vessel into the house of Jehovah. ASV

Jeremiah 11:17

For Jehovah of hosts, who planted thee, hath pronounced evil against thee, because of the evil of the house of Israel and of the house of Judah, which they have wrought for themselves in provoking me to anger by offering incense unto Baal. ASV

Jeremiah 14:12

When they fast, I will not hear their cry; and when they offer burnt-offering and meal-offering, I will not accept them; but I will consume them by the sword, and by the famine, and by the pestilence. ASV

Ezekiel 40:38

And a chamber with the door thereof was by the posts at the gates; there they washed the burnt-offering. ASV

Ezekiel 40:39

And in the porch of the gate were two tables on this side, and two tables on that side, to slay thereon the burnt-offering and the sin-offering and the trespass-offering. ASV

Ezekiel 40:42

And there were four tables for the burnt-offering, of hewn stone, a cubit and a half long, and a cubit and a half broad, and one cubit high; whereupon they laid the instruments wherewith they slew the burnt-offering and the sacrifice. ASV

Ezekiel 40:43

And the hooks, a handbreadth long, were fastened within round about: and upon the tables was the flesh of the oblation. ASV

Ezekiel 42:13

Then said he unto me, The north chambers and the south chambers, which are before the separate place, they are the holy chambers, where the priests that are near unto Jehovah shall eat the most holy things: there shall they lay the most holy things, and the meal-offering, and the sin-offering, and the trespass-offering; for the place is holy. ASV

Ezekiel 43:19

Thou shalt give to the priests the Levites that are of the seed of Zadok, who are near unto me, to minister unto me, saith the Lord Jehovah, a young bullock for a sin-offering. ASV

Ezekiel 43:21

Thou shalt also take the bullock of the sin-offering, and it shall be burnt in the appointed place of the house, without the sanctuary. ASV

Ezekiel 43:22

And on the second day thou shalt offer a he-goat without blemish for a sin-offering; and they shall cleanse the altar, as they did cleanse it with the bullock. ASV

Ezekiel 43:24

And thou shalt bring them near before Jehovah, and the priests shall cast salt upon them, and they shall offer them up for a burnt-offering unto Jehovah. ASV

Ezekiel 43:25

Seven days shalt thou prepare every day a goat for a sin-offering: they shall also prepare a young bullock, and a ram out of the flock, without blemish. ASV

Ezekiel 44:11

Yet they shall be ministers in my sanctuary, having oversight at the gates of the house, and ministering in the house: they shall slay the burnt-offering and the sacrifice for the people, and they shall stand before them to minister unto them. ASV

Ezekiel 44:27

And in the day that he goeth into the sanctuary, into the inner court, to minister in the sanctuary, he shall offer his sin-offering, saith the Lord Jehovah. ASV

Ezekiel 44:29

They shall eat the meal-offering, and the sin-offering, and the trespass-offering; and every devoted thing in Israel shall be theirs. ASV

Ezekiel 45:17

And it shall be the prince's part to give the burnt-offerings, and the meal-offerings, and the drink-offerings, in the feasts, and on the new moons, and on the sabbaths, in all the appointed feasts of the house of Israel: he shall prepare the sin-offering, and the meal-offering, and the burnt-offering, and the peace-offerings, to make atonement for the house of Israel. ASV

Ezekiel 45:19

And the priest shall take of the blood of the sin-offering, and put it upon the door-posts of the house, and upon the four corners of the ledge of the altar, and upon the posts of the gate of the inner court. ASV

Ezekiel 45:22

And upon that day shall the prince prepare for himself and for all the people of the land a bullock for a sin-offering. ASV

Ezekiel 45:23

And the seven days of the feast he shall prepare a burnt-offering to Jehovah, seven bullocks and seven rams without blemish daily the seven days; and a he-goat daily for a sin-offering. ASV

Ezekiel 45:24

And he shall prepare a meal-offering, an ephah for a bullock, and an ephah for a ram, and a hin of oil to an ephah. ASV

Ezekiel 45:25

In the seventh (month), in the fifteenth day of the month, in the feast, shall he do the like the seven days; according to the sin-offering, according to the burnt-offering, and according to the meal-offering, and according to the oil. ASV

Ezekiel 46:2

And the prince shall enter by the way of the porch of the gate without, and shall stand by the post of the gate; and the priests shall prepare his burnt-offering and his peace-offerings, and he shall worship at the threshold of the gate: then he shall go forth; but the gate shall not be shut until the evening. ASV

Ezekiel 46:4

And the burnt-offering that the prince shall offer unto Jehovah shall be on the sabbath day six lambs without blemish and a ram without blemish; ASV

Ezekiel 46:5

And the meal-offering shall be an ephah for the ram, and the meal-offering for the lambs as he is able to give, and a hin of oil to an ephah. ASV

Ezekiel 46:7

And he shall prepare a meal-offering, an ephah for the bullock, and an ephah for the ram, and for the lambs according as he is able, and a hin of oil to an ephah. ASV

Ezekiel 46:11

And in the feasts and in the solemnities the meal-offering shall be an ephah for a bullock, and an ephah for a ram, and for the lambs as he is able to give, and a hin of oil to an ephah. ASV

Ezekiel 46:12

And when the prince shall prepare a freewill-offering, a burnt-offering or peace-offerings as a freewill-offering unto Jehovah, one shall open for him the gate that looketh toward

the east; and he shall prepare his burnt-offering and his peace-offerings, as he doth on the sabbath day: then he shall go forth; and after his going forth one shall shut the gate. ASV

Ezekiel 46:13

And thou shalt prepare a lamb a year old without blemish for a burnt-offering unto Jehovah daily: morning by morning shalt thou prepare it. ASV

Ezekiel 46:14

And thou shalt prepare a meal-offering with it morning by morning, the sixth part of an ephah, and the third part of a hin of oil, to moisten the fine flour; a meal-offering unto Jehovah continually by a perpetual ordinance. ASV

Ezekiel 46:15

Thus shall they prepare the lamb, and the meal-offering, and the oil, morning by morning, for a continual burnt-offering. ASV

Ezekiel 46:20

And he said unto me, This is the place where the priests shall boil the trespass-offering and the sin-offering, (and) where they shall bake the meal-offering; that they bring them not forth into the outer court, to sanctify the people. ASV

Ezekiel 48:8

And by the border of Judah, from the east side unto the west side, shall be the oblation which ye shall offer, five and twenty thousand (reeds) in breadth, and in length as one of the portions, from the east side unto the west side: and the sanctuary shall be in the midst of it. ASV

Joel 1:9

The meal-offering and the drink-offering are cut off from the house of Jehovah; the priests, Jehovah's ministers, mourn. ASV

Joel 1:13

Gird yourselves (with sackcloth), and lament, ye priests; wail, ye ministers of the altar; come, lie all night in sackcloth, ye ministers of my God: for the meal-offering and the drink-offering are withholden from the house of your God. ASV

Joel 2:14

Who knoweth whether he will not turn and repent, and leave a blessing behind him, even a meal-offering and a drink-offering unto Jehovah your God? ASV

Zephaniah 3:10

From beyond the rivers of Ethiopia my suppliants, even the daughter of my dispersed, shall bring mine offering. ASV

Malachi 1:10

Oh that there were one among you that would shut the doors, that ye might not kindle (fire on) mine altar in vain! I have no pleasure in you, saith Jehovah of hosts, neither will I accept an offering at your hand. ASV

Malachi 1:11

For from the rising of the sun even unto the going down of the same my name (shall be) great among the Gentiles; and in every place incense (shall be) offered unto my name, and a pure offering: for my name (shall be) great among the Gentiles, saith Jehovah of hosts. ASV

Malachi 1:13

Ye say also, Behold, what a weariness is it! and ye have snuffed at it, saith Jehovah of hosts; and ye have brought that which was taken by violence, and the lame, and the sick; thus ye bring the offering: should I accept this at your hand? saith Jehovah. ASV

Malachi 2:12

Jehovah will cut off, to the man that doeth this, him that waketh and him that answereth, out of the tents of Jacob, and him that offereth an offering unto Jehovah of hosts. ASV

Malachi 2:13

And this again ye do: ye cover the altar of Jehovah with tears, with weeping, and with sighing, insomuch that he regardeth not the offering any more, neither receiveth it with good will at your hand. ASV

Malachi 3:3

And he will sit as a refiner and purifier of silver, and he will purify the sons of Levi, and refine them as gold and silver; and they shall offer unto Jehovah offerings in righteousness. ASV

Malachi 3:4

Then shall the offering of Judah and Jerusalem be pleasant unto Jehovah, as in the days of old, and as in ancient years. ASV

Luke 23:36

And the soldiers also mocked him, coming to him, offering him vinegar, ASV

Acts 21:26

Then Paul took the men, and the next day purifying himself with them went into the temple, declaring the fulfilment of the days of purification, until the offering was offered for every one of them. ASV

Romans 15:16

That I should be a minister of Christ Jesus unto the Gentiles, ministering the gospel of God, that the offering up of the Gentiles might be made acceptable, being sanctified by the Holy Spirit. ASV

Ephesians 5:2

And walk in love, even as Christ also loved you, and gave himself up for us, an offering and a sacrifice to God for an odor of a sweet smell. ASV

Hebrews 10:5

Wherefore when he cometh into the world, he saith, Sacrifice and offering thou wouldest not, But a body didst thou prepare for me; ASV

Hebrews 10:10

By which will we have been sanctified through the offering of the body of Jesus Christ once for all. ASV

Hebrews 10:11

And every priest indeed standeth day by day ministering and offering oftentimes the same sacrifices, the which can never take away sins: ASV

Hebrews 10:14

For by one offering he hath perfected for ever them that are sanctified. ASV

Hebrews 10:18

Now where remission of these is, there is no more offering for sin. ASV

Offerings

Ezekiel 43:27

And when they have accomplished the days, it shall be that upon the eighth day, and forward, the priests shall make your burnt-offerings upon the altar, and your peace-offerings; and I will accept you, saith the Lord Jehovah. ASV

Ezekiel 45:15

And one lamb of the flock, out of two hundred, from the well-watered pastures of Israel; — for a meal-offering, and for a burnt-offering, and for peace-offerings, to make atonement for them, saith the Lord Jehovah. ASV

Ezekiel 45:17

And it shall be the prince's part to give the burnt-offerings, and the meal-offerings, and the drink-offerings, in the feasts, and on the new moons, and on the sabbaths, in all the appointed feasts of the house of Israel: he shall prepare the sin-offering, and the meal-offering, and the burnt-offering, and the peace-offerings, to make atonement for the house of Israel. ASV

Ezekiel 46:2

And the prince shall enter by the way of the porch of the gate without, and shall stand by the post of the gate; and the priests shall prepare his burnt-offering and his peace-offerings, and he shall worship at the threshold of the gate: then he shall go forth; but the gate shall not be shut until the evening. ASV

Ezekiel 46:12

And when the prince shall prepare a freewill-offering, a burnt-offering or peace-offerings as a freewill-offering unto Jehovah, one shall open for him the gate that looketh toward the east; and he shall prepare his burnt-offering and his peace-offerings, as he doth on the sabbath day: then he shall go forth; and after his going forth one shall shut the gate. ASV

Hosea 6:6

For I desire goodness, and not sacrifice; and the knowledge of God more than burnt-offerings. ASV

Hosea 8:13

As for the sacrifices of mine offerings, they sacrifice flesh and eat it; but Jehovah accepteth them not: now will he remember their iniquity, and visit their sins; they shall return to Egypt. ASV

Hosea 9:4

They shall not pour out wineofferings) to Jehovah, neither shall they be pleasing unto him: their sacrifices shall be unto them as the bread of mourners; all that eat thereof shall be polluted; for their bread shall be for their appetite; it shall not come into the house of Jehovah. ASV

Amos 4:5

And offer a sacrifice of thanksgiving of that which is leavened, and proclaim freewill-offerings and publish them: for this pleaseth you, O ye children of Israel, saith the Lord Jehovah. ASV

Amos 5:22

Yea, though ye offer me your burnt-offerings and meal-offerings, I will not accept them; neither will I regard the peace-offerings of your fat beasts. ASV

Amos 5:25

Did ye bring unto me sacrifices and offerings in the wilderness forty years, O house of Israel? ASV

Micah 6:6

Wherewith shall I come before Jehovah, and bow myself before the high God? shall I come before him with burnt-offerings, with calves a year old? ASV

Malachi 3:8

Will a man rob God? yet ye rob me. But ye say, Wherein have we robbed thee? In tithes and offerings. ASV

Mark 12:33

And to love him with all the heart, and with all the understanding, and with all the strength, and to love his neighbor as himself, is much more than all whole burnt-offerings and sacrifices. ASV

Luke 21:4

For all these did of their superfluity cast in unto the gifts; but she of her want did cast in all the living that she had. ASV

Acts 24:17

Now after some years I came to bring alms to my nation, and offerings: ASV

1 Corinthians 9:13

Know ye not that they that minister about sacred things eat (of) the things of the temple, (and) they that wait upon the altar have their portion with the altar? ASV

Hebrews 10:6

In whole burnt offerings and (sacrifices) for sin thou hadst no pleasure: ASV

Hebrews 10:8

Saying above, Sacrifices and offerings and whole burnt offerings and (sacrifices) for sin thou wouldest not, neither hadst pleasure therein (the which are offered according to the law), ASV

Summary

The Scriptures illustrate that giving of one's own things is an evidence of God's grace in a person's life (II Corinthians 8:4-7). Because 100 percent of what is received comes from God, we are responsible to use it wisely and in accordance with God's will. Like every other area of stewardship, God is interested in the whole picture, not just a percentage. What a person does with all his treasure is important to God.

According to the Scriptures, the personal handling of financial related issues, and personal stewardship means recognizing our obligations to God because of Calvary. Stewardship means that God owns you and is counting on you to become an instrument through which He can love and save the world. It's as simple as that! If you cannot offer yourself as a channel of God's wealth, how can He bless your life? The bottom line in stewardship is not money or a block of time, but your entire life.

The person who takes stewardship seriously will regard his or her life, talents, strength and money as a trust from God. Trustees have specific responsibilities. They are charged with holding property in trust for someone else.

Scriptural principles give us clues as to how we can trust God with our money and our entire lives. Four steps may help simplify the process.

Placing God First

The first step is to put God first and He will supply our basic needs. A Christian should be content with having his needs met when he learns how to surrender all control of his life to God. Then God can entrust more responsibility to him.

"But seek first his kingdom and his righteousness, and all these things will be given to you as well" (Matthew 6:33 NIV).

Trusting God's Provision

A second step is to trust God to provide for financial provision. We will probably experience both plentiful and lean times financially, for such is life; but if we will be faithful and not complain, we can be sure that God will provide.

God's Desire to Bless

Thirdly, God will care for our needs and He will even give us the desires of our hearts. According to Psalm 37:4, God enjoys giving to those He loves. We are directed to have fun (delight ourselves in the Lord) and are reminded that He loves us so much that He will just give us the principled desires of our heart.

Responsible with Finances

And finally, Jesus taught that we must be responsible in our finances. God is the source of all wealth. He is the original owner of all things, for He made all things. As Scripture has said, He owns the cattle on a thousand hills. God also gives us the ability to earn a living (Deuteronomy 8:18).

Really, all that we have or expect to obtain comes from God. Our clothes, cars, homes and jobs are ultimately all gifts from His bountiful hand. God is not stingy or tight-fisted, nor does He refuse to share with mankind what is rightfully His.

Jesus also taught us that mankind is on earth for a very, very short time and then goes to an eternal destination. If we really understand this to be true, where we place our priorities and how we deal with our finances is extremely important. Should our resources be physical and temporal or spiritual and eternal? What is a man's real treasure? Matthew gives us a very concise answer to this question.

> *"But store up for yourselves treasures in heaven, where moth and rust do not destroy, and where thieves do not break in and steal. For where your treasure is, there your heart will be also"* (Matthew 6:20, 21 NIV).

What are man's real treasures—that which thieves can steal and corrupt, or that which becomes part of our retirement plan in heaven? "For where your treasure is, there will your heart be also" (Matthew 6:21 NIV).

All the Financial Scriptures in the Bible with Commentary

Source Material

21 Unbreakable Laws of Success, Max Anders, Thomas Nelson, 1996
A Christian Guide to Prosperity; Fries & Taylor, California: Communications Research, 1984
A Look At Stewardship, Word Aflame Publications, 2001
American Savings Education Council (http://www.asec.org)
Anointed For Business, Ed Silvoso, Regal, 2002
Avoiding Common Financial Mistakes, Ron Blue, Navpress, 1991
Baker Encyclopedia of the Bible; Walter Elwell, Michigan: Baker Book House, 1988
Becoming The Best, Barry Popplewell, England: Gower Publishing Company Limited, 1988
Business Proverbs, Steve Marr, Fleming H. Revell, 2001
Cheapskate Monthly, Mary Hunt
Commentary on the Old Testament; Keil Delitzsch, Michigan: Eerdmans Publishing, 1986
Crown Financial Ministries, various publications
Customers As Partners, Chip Bell, Texas: Berrett Koehler Publishers, 1994
Cut Your Bills in Half; Pennsylvania: Rodale Press, Inc., 1989
Debt-Free Living, Larry Burkett, Dimensions, 2001
Die Broke, Stephen M. Pollan & Mark Levine, HarperBusiness, 1997
Double Your Profits, Bob Fifer, Virginia: Lincoln Hall Press, 1993
Eerdmans' Handbook to the Bible, Michigan: William B. Eerdmans Publishing Company, 1987
Eight Steps to Seven Figures, Charles B. Carlson, Double Day, 2000
Everyday Life in Bible Times; Washington DC: National Geographic Society, 1967
Financial Dominion, Norvel Hayes, Harrison House, 1986
Financial Freedom, Larry Burkett, Moody Press, 1991
Financial Freedom, Patrick Clements, VMI Publishers, 2003
Financial Peace, Dave Ramsey, Viking Press, 2003
Financial Self-Defense; Charles Givens, New York: Simon And Schuster, 1990
Flood Stage, Oral Roberts, 1981
Generous Living, Ron Blue, Zondervan, 1997
Get It All Done, Tony and Robbie Fanning, New York:Pennsylvania: Chilton Book, 1979
Getting Out of Debt, Howard Dayton, Tyndale House, 1986

All the Financial Scriptures in the Bible With Commentary

Getting Out of Debt, Mary Stephenson, Fact Sheet 436, University of Maryland Cooperative Extension Service, 1988
Giving and Tithing, Larry Burkett, Moody Press, 1991
God's Plan For Giving, John MacArthur, Jr., Moody Press, 1985
God's Will is Prosperity, Gloria Copeland, Harrison House, 1978
Great People of the Bible and How They Lived; New York: Reader's Digest, 1974
How Others Can Help You Get Out of Debt; Esther M. Maddux, Circular 759-3,
How To Make A Business Plan That Works, Henderson, North Island Sound Limited, 1989
How To Manage Your Money, Larry Burkett, Moody Press, 1999
How to Personally Profit From the Laws of Success, Sterling Sill, NIFP, Inc., 1978
How to Plan for Your Retirement; New York: Corrigan & Kaufman, Longmeadow Press, 1985
Is God Your Source?, Oral Roberts, 1992
It's Not Luck, Eliyahu Goldratt, Great Barrington, MA: The North River Press, 1994
Jesus CEO, Laurie Beth Jones, Hyperion, 1995
John Avanzini Answers Your Questions About Biblical Economics, Harrison House, 1992
Living on Less and Liking It More, Maxine Hancock, Chicago, Illinois: Moody Press, 1976
Making It Happen; Charles Conn, New Jersey: Fleming H. Revell Company, 1981
Master Your Money Or It Will Master You, Arlo E. Moehlenpah, Doing Good Ministries, 1999
Master Your Money; Ron Blue, Tennessee: Thomas Nelson, Inc. 1986
Miracle of Seed Faith, Oral Roberts, 1970
Mississippi State University Extension Service
Money, Possessions, and Eternity, Randy Alcorn, Tyndale House, 2003
More Than Enough, David Ramsey, Penguin Putnam Inc, 2002
Moving the Hand of God, John Avanzini, Harrison House, 1990
Multiplication, Tommy Barnett, Creation House, 1997
NebFacts, Nebraska Cooperative Extension
New York Post
One Up On Wall Street; New York: Peter Lynch, Simon And Schuster, 1989
Personal Finances, Larry Burkett, Moody Press, 1991
Portable MBA in Finance and Accounting; Livingstone, Canada: John Wiley & Sons, Inc., 1992
Principle Centered Leadership, Stephen R. Covey, New York: Summit Books, 1991
Principles of Financial Management, Kolb & DeMong, Texas: Business Publications, Inc., 1988
Rapid Debt Reduction Strategies, John Avanzini, HIS Publishing, 1990
Real Wealth, Wade Cook, Arizona: Regency Books, 1985
See You At The Top, Zig Ziglar, Louisianna: Pelican Publishing Company, 1977

Sources

Seed Faith Commentary on the Holy Bible, Oral Roberts, Pinoak Publications, 1975
Sharkproof, Harvey Mackay, New York: HarperCollins Publishers, 1993
Smart Money, Ken and Daria Dolan, New York: Random House, Inc., 1988
Strong's Concordance, Tennessee: Crusade Bible Publishers, Inc.,
Success by Design, Peter Hirsch, Bethany House, 2002
Success is the Quality of your Journey, Jennifer James, New York: Newmarket Press, 1983
Swim with the Sharks Without Being Eaten Alive, Harvey Mackay, William Morrow , 1988
The Almighty and the Dollar; Jim McKeever, Oregon: Omega Publications, 1981
The Challenge, Robert Allen, New York: Simon And Schuster, 1987
The Family Financial Workbook, Larry Burkett, Moody Press, 2002
The Management Methods of Jesus, Bob Briner, Thomas Nelson, 1996
The Millionaire Next Door, Thomas Stanley & William Danko, Pocket Books, 1996
The Money Book for Kids, Nancy Burgeson, Troll Associates,1992
The Money Book for King's Kids; Harold E. Hill, New Jersey: Fleming H. Revell Company, 1984
The Seven Habits of Highly Effective People, Stephen Covey, New York: Simon And Schuster, 1989
The Wealthy Barber, David Chilton, California: Prima Publishing, 1991
Theological Wordbook of the Old Testament, Chicago, Illinois: Moody Press, 1981
Treasury of Courage and Confidence, Norman Vincent Peale, New York: Doubleday & Co., 1970
True Prosperity, Dick Iverson, Bible Temple Publishing, 1993
Trust God For Your Finances, Jack Hartman, Lamplight Publications, 1983
University of Georgia Cooperative Extension Service, 1985
Virginia Cooperative Extension
Webster's Unabridged Dictionary, Dorset & Baber, 1983
What Is an Entrepreneur; David Robinson, MA: Kogan Page Limited, 1990
Word Meanings in the New Testament, Ralph Earle, Michigan: Baker Book House, 1986
Word Pictures in the New Testament; Robertson, Michigan: Baker Book House, 1930
Word Studies in the New Testament; Vincent, New York: Charles Scribner's Sons, 1914
Worth
You Can Be Financially Free, George Fooshee, Jr., 1976, Fleming H. Revell Company.
Your Key to God's Bank, Rex Humbard, 1977
Your Money Counts, Howard, Dayton, Tyndale House, 1997
Your Money Management, MaryAnn Paynter, Circular 1271, University of Illinois Cooperative Extension Service, 1987.
Your Money Matters, Malcolm MacGregor, Bethany Fellowship, Inc., 1977
Your Road to Recovery, Oral Roberts, Oliver Nelson, 1986

Comments On Sources

Over the years I have collected bits and pieces of interesting material, written notes on sermons I've heard, jotted down comments on financial articles I've read, and gathered a lot of great information. It is unfortunate that I didn't record the sources of all of these notes in my earlier years. I gratefully extend my appreciation to the many writers, authors, teachers and pastors from whose articles and sermons I have gleaned much insight.

Rich Brott

Online Resources

American Savings Education Council (http://www.asec.org)
Bloomberg.com (http://www.bloomberg.com)
Bureau of the Public Debt Online (http://www.publicdebt.treas.gov)
BusinessWeek (http://www.businessweek.com)
Charles Schwab & Co., Inc. (http://www.schwab.com)
Consumer Federation of America (http://www.consumerfed.org)
Debt Advice.org (http://www.debtadvice.org)
Federal Reserve System (http://www.federalreserve.gov)
Fidelity Investments (http://www.fidelity.com)
Financial Planning Association (http://www.fpanet.org)
Forbes (www.forbes.com)
Fortune Magazine (http://www.fortune.com)
Generous Giving (http://www.generousgiving.org/)
Investing for Your Future (http://www.investing.rutgers.edu)
Kiplinger Magazine (http://www.kiplinger.com/)
Money Magazine (http://money.cnn.com)
MorningStar (http://www.morningstar.com)
MSN Money (http://moneycentral.msn.com)
Muriel Siebert (http://www.siebertnet.com)
National Center on Education and the Economy (http://www.ncee.org)
National Foundation for Credit Counseling (http://www.nfcc.org)
Quicken (http://www.quicken.com)
Smart Money (http://www.smartmoney.com)
Social Security Online (http://www.ssa.gov)
Standard & Poor's (http://www2.standardandpoors.com)
The Dollar Stretcher, Gary Foreman, (http://www.stretcher.com)
The Vanguard Group (http://flagship.vanguard.com)
U.S. Securities and Exchange Commission (http://www.sec.gov)
Yahoo! Finance (http://finance.yahoo.com)

Magazine Resources

Business Week
Consumer Reports
Forbes
Kiplinger's Personal Finance
Money
Smart Money
US News and World Report

Newspaper Resources

Barrons
Investors Business Daily
USA Today
Wall Street Journal
Washington Times

Additional Resources by Rich Brott

5 Simple Keys to Financial Freedom

Change Your Life Forever!

By Rich Brott

6" x 9", 108 pages
ISBN 1-60185-022-0
ISBN (EAN) 978-1-60185-022-5

a b c
Book Publishing

Order online at:
www.amazon.com
www.barnesandnoble.com
www.booksamillion.com
www.citychristianpublishing.com
www.bordersstores.com

www.AbcBookPublishing.com

Additional Resources by Rich Brott

10 Life-Changing Attitudes That Will Make You a Financial Success

By Rich Brott

6" x 9", 108 pages
ISBN 1-60185-021-2
ISBN (EAN) 978-1-60185-021-8

abc Book Publishing

Order online at:
www.amazon.com
www.barnesandnoble.com
www.booksamillion.com
www.citychristianpublishing.com
www.bordersstores.com

www.AbcBookPublishing.com

Additional Resources by Rich Brott

15 Biblical Responsibilities Leading to Financial Wisdom

Accepting Personal Accountability

By Rich Brott

6" x 9", 120 pages
ISBN 1-60185-010-7
ISBN (EAN) 978-1-60185-010-2

Order online at:
www.amazon.com
www.barnesandnoble.com
www.booksamillion.com
www.citychristianpublishing.com
www.bordersstores.com

abc Book Publishing

www.AbcBookPublishing.com

Additional Resources by Rich Brott

30 Biblical Principles for Managing Your Money

Insights that Will Set You Free!

By Rich Brott

6" x 9", 160 pages
ISBN 1-60185-012-3
ISBN (EAN) 978-1-60185-012-6

Book Publishing

Order online at:
www.amazon.com
www.barnesandnoble.com
www.booksamillion.com
www.citychristianpublishing.com
www.bordersstores.com

www.AbcBookPublishing.com

Additional Resources by Rich Brott

35 Keys to Financial Independence

Finding the Freedom You Seek!

By Rich Brott

6" x 9", 176 pages
ISBN 1-60185-020-4
ISBN (EAN) 978-1-60185-020-1

Order online at:
www.amazon.com
www.barnesandnoble.com
www.booksamillion.com
www.citychristianpublishing.com
www.bordersstores.com

abc Book Publishing

www.AbcBookPublishing.com

Additional Resources by Rich Brott

A Biblical Perspective on Tithing & Giving

A Believer's Stewardship Guide

By Rich Brott

6" x 9", 172 pages
ISBN 1-60185-000-X
ISBN (EAN) 978-1-60185-000-3

Book Publishing

Order online at:
www.amazon.com
www.barnesandnoble.com
www.booksamillion.com
www.citychristianpublishing.com
www.bordersstores.com

www.AbcBookPublishing.com

Additional Resources by Rich Brott

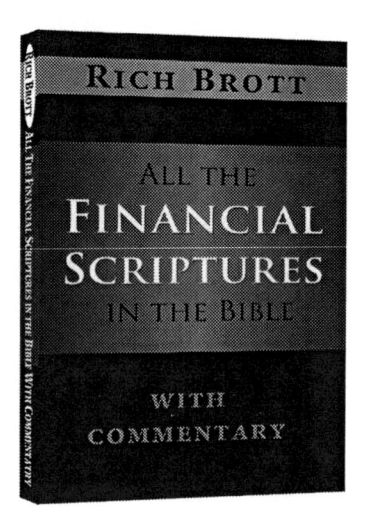

All the Financial Scriptures in the Bible with Commentary

By Rich Brott

6" x 9", 364 pages
ISBN 1-60185-004-2
ISBN (EAN) 978-1-60185-004-1

Book Publishing

Order online at:
www.amazon.com
www.barnesandnoble.com
www.booksamillion.com
www.citychristianpublishing.com
www.bordersstores.com

www.AbcBookPublishing.com

Additional Resources by Rich Brott

Basic Principles for Maximizing Your Personal Cash Flow

7 Steps to Financial Freedom!

By Rich Brott

6" x 9", 120 pages
ISBN 1-60185-019-0
ISBN (EAN) 978-1-60185-019-5

Book Publishing

Order online at:
www.amazon.com
www.barnesandnoble.com
www.booksamillion.com
www.citychristianpublishing.com
www.bordersstores.com

www.AbcBookPublishing.com

Additional Resources by Rich Brott

Basic Principles of Conservative Investing

9 Principles You Must Follow

By Rich Brott

6" x 9", 116 pages
ISBN 1-60185-018-2
ISBN (EAN) 978-1-60185-018-8

abc Book Publishing

Order online at:
www.amazon.com
www.barnesandnoble.com
www.booksamillion.com
www.citychristianpublishing.com
www.bordersstores.com

www.AbcBookPublishing.com

Additional Resources by Rich Brott

Biblical Principles for Achieving Personal Success

8 Critical Insights You Must Discover!

By Rich Brott

6" x 9", 248 pages
ISBN 1-60185-013-1
ISBN (EAN) 978-1-60185-013-3

abc Book Publishing

Order online at:
www.amazon.com
www.barnesandnoble.com
www.booksamillion.com
www.citychristianpublishing.com
www.bordersstores.com

www.AbcBookPublishing.com

Additional Resources by Rich Brott

Biblical Principles for Staying Out of Debt

7 Things You Must Know!

By Rich Brott

6" x 9", 120 pages
ISBN 1-60185-009-3
ISBN (EAN) 978-1-60185-009-6

abc Book Publishing

Order online at:
www.amazon.com
www.barnesandnoble.com
www.booksamillion.com
www.citychristianpublishing.com
www.bordersstores.com

www.AbcBookPublishing.com

Additional Resources by Rich Brott

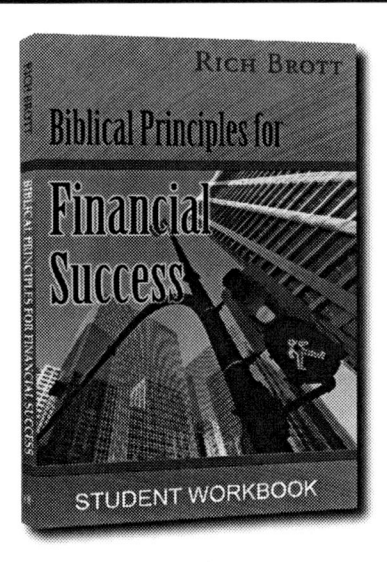

Biblical Principles for Financial Success

Student Workbook

By Rich Brott

7.5" x 9.25", 228 pages
ISBN 1-60185-016-6
ISBN (EAN) 978-1-60185-016-4

Book Publishing

Order online at:
www.amazon.com
www.barnesandnoble.com
www.booksamillion.com
www.citychristianpublishing.com
www.bordersstores.com

www.AbcBookPublishing.com

Additional Resources by Rich Brott

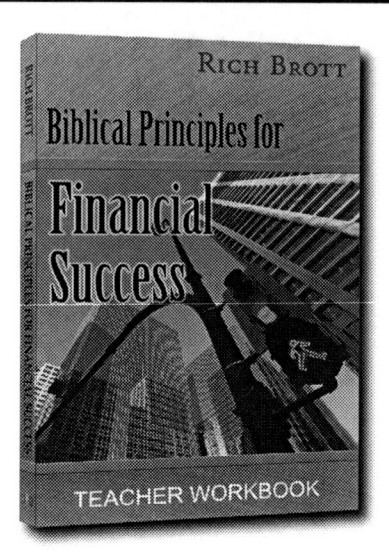

Biblical Principles for Financial Success

Teacher Workbook

By Rich Brott

7.5" x 9.25", 228 pages
ISBN 1-60185-015-8
ISBN (EAN) 978-1-60185-015-7

Book Publishing

Order online at:
www.amazon.com
www.barnesandnoble.com
www.booksamillion.com
www.citychristianpublishing.com
www.bordersstores.com

www.AbcBookPublishing.com

Additional Resources by Rich Brott

Biblical Principles that Create Success through Productivity

How God Blesses Our Work Ethic

By Rich Brott

6" x 9", 224 pages
ISBN 1-60185-007-7
ISBN (EAN) 978-1-60185-007-2

abc Book Publishing

Order online at:
www.amazon.com
www.barnesandnoble.com
www.booksamillion.com
www.citychristianpublishing.com
www.bordersstores.com

www.AbcBookPublishing.com

Additional Resources by Rich Brott

Business, Occupations, Professions & Vocations in the Bible

By Rich Brott

6" x 9", 212 pages
ISBN 1-60185-014-X
ISBN (EAN) 978-1-60185-014-0

abc Book Publishing

Order online at:
www.amazon.com
www.barnesandnoble.com
www.booksamillion.com
www.citychristianpublishing.com
www.bordersstores.com

www.AbcBookPublishing.com

Additional Resources by Rich Brott

Biblical Principles for Success in Personal Finance

Your Roadmap to Financial Independence

By Rich Brott

7.5" x 10", 519 pages
ISBN 0-914936-72-7
ISBN (EAN) 978-0-914936-72-5

Book Publishing

Order online at:
www.amazon.com
www.barnesandnoble.com
www.booksamillion.com
www.citychristianpublishing.com
www.bordersstores.com

www.AbcBookPublishing.com

Additional Resources by Rich Brott

Biblical Principles for Building a Successful Business

A Practical Guide to Assessing, Evaluating, and Growing a Successful Cutting-Edge Enterprise in Today's Business Environment

By Rich Brott & Frank Damazio

7.5" x 10", 477 pages
ISBN 1-59383-027-0
ISBN (EAN) 978-1-59383-027-4

abc Book Publishing

Order online at:
www.amazon.com
www.barnesandnoble.com
www.booksamillion.com
www.citychristianpublishing.com
www.bordersstores.com

www.AbcBookPublishing.com

Additional Resources by Rich Brott

Biblical Principles for Becoming Debt Free!

Rescue Your Life and Liberate Your Future!

By Rich Brott & Frank Damazio

7.5" x 10", 320 pages
ISBN 1-886849-85-4
ISBN 978-1-886849-85-3

abc Book Publishing

Order online at:
www.amazon.com
www.barnesandnoble.com
www.booksamillion.com
www.citychristianpublishing.com
www.bordersstores.com

www.AbcBookPublishing.com

Additional Resources by Rich Brott

Biblical Principles for Releasing Financial Provision!

Obtaining the Favor of God in Your Personal and Business World

By Rich Brott

7.5" x 10", 456 pages
ISBN 1-59383-021-1
ISBN (EAN) 978-1-59383-021-2

a b c
Book Publishing

Order online at:
www.amazon.com
www.barnesandnoble.com
www.booksamillion.com
www.citychristianpublishing.com
www.bordersstores.com

www.AbcBookPublishing.com

Additional Resources by Rich Brott

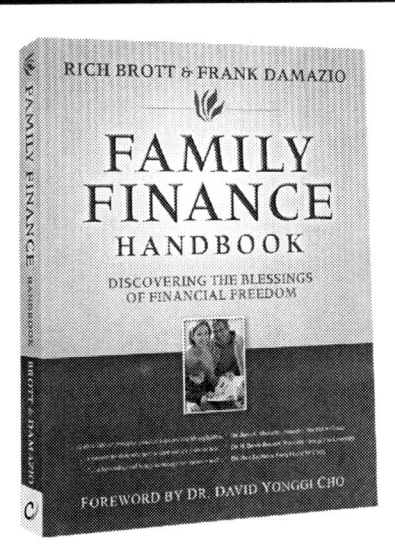

Family Finance Handbook

*Discovering the Blessing
of Financial Freedom*

By Rich Brott & Frank Damazio

7.5" x 10", 288 pages
ISBN 1-914936-60-3
ISBN 978-1-914936-60-2

abc Book Publishing

Order online at:
www.amazon.com
www.barnesandnoble.com
www.booksamillion.com
www.citychristianpublishing.com
www.bordersstores.com

www.AbcBookPublishing.com